# For The Love of Beirut

*Samuel T. Eloud*

## Samuel Toufic Eloud

# DEDICATION

*This book is dedicated to my family and friends, living and deceased, who along with me endured the terrors of a horrible war which displaced many Lebanese, sending them into exile from their beloved homeland.*

.

# CONTENTS

How shall I go in peace and without sorrow?  Nay, not without a wound
in the spirit shall I leave this city.


----from *The Prophet*
by Kahlil Gibran, 1923

# PROLOGUE

There was no one standing in the parking lot. I could see my car there, but the lot looked fairly empty. As I turned my head to walk back into the Armed Forces Recruiting Station, I could see a sniper on the roof of the end store in the strip mall. I could also hear a single engine Cessna circling overhead.

I went back inside, picked up the phone, and asked the hostage negotiator what he wanted me to do next. He said to walk outside into the parking lot with my hands over my head and there would be an officer who would instruct me as to what to do next. So, I said it had been nice talking to him and he said the same to me. As I hung up the phone, I noticed that the eleven bullets I had set up along the desk were still there. I shrugged and walked outside.

When I got out of the recruiting station, I saw that the AK-47 and the 25 caliber pistol I had placed on the ground had been removed. With my hands resting on the back of my head, I crossed into the parking lot. A detective dressed in a gray blazer and slacks motioned to me to step forward and walk towards him.

As I walked towards him, I could see the media frenzy on the outskirts of the parking lot. Fire trucks were blocking West Broad Street, their lights flashing. I was relieved the media was there because if anything went wrong, there would be proof that I had done as I was told.

After I got on my knees and put my hands behind my back as he instructed me, he gently put the handcuffs on my wrists and helped me stand up. Immediately thereafter, an old, unmarked white van pulled up next to us. He removed the padlock on the door while asking me if I was okay. I replied that I was.

I stepped inside the van, a windowless steel box with benches down each side. The only opening was a small rectangle of mesh through which I could see the driver and the police officer next to him who frequently looked back to check on me. Uncomfortable with the handcuffs behind my back in the moving van, I decided to slide my legs through my arms, bringing my hands in front of me. The police officer looked at me, noticing my handcuffs were now in the front.

I just looked at him and smiled because I didn't care what happened next. I leaned back and rested my head against the cool steel wall of the van. I had survived Beirut, I thought to myself. I can survive anything.

Even this.

Part I
1968-1986

# Chapter 1
## Fort Worth to Beirut

My name is Samuel Eloud and I'm writing my life story to show you how different it is to grow up in the Middle East as an American citizen with Lebanese parents. My home was Beirut, Lebanon, a most notorious place, a place often in the news. My father, Toufic Eloud, was a pilot for Air Jordan and my mother, Yester Topalian Eloud, a housewife. In 1968, my mother accompanied my dad to Fort Worth, Texas, where he received training to fly Boeing 747s for his new job with Trans Mediterranean Airways. While there, my mother gave birth to me, her first child, on May 6, 1968. Two months later, they flew back to Lebanon with me, a U.S. citizen.

I remember how beautiful it was as a child living near the blue Mediterranean. Most people think that Lebanon is dry and desert-like with camels running around, something I've been asked about a thousand times. So, I stop and tell them that it is the most beautiful place on earth, the hills covered with green, the most beautiful green vegetation, and that the sea is a blue like no other body of water. From the shores of the Mediterranean, it is only an hour's drive to the mountains of Lebanon, an elevation of ten thousand feet. So, all in one day you can ski in knee-deep powdery snow around the famous Cedars of Lebanon and then drive back down to the shores of the Mediterranean and get a suntan. These pleasant memories are few because when I was seven years old all hell broke loose and a bloody civil war started.

The days of the Paris of Lebanon were over; now it was door-to-door shooting between the Palestinians, the Lebanese Army, the

Christians, the Muslims, and the Druze. Now every neighborhood was fighting, intense door-to-door fighting that brought fear and terror to every household. People who had grown up together were killing each other left and right. Even now, as an adult, I can hear the cannons firing shells every five seconds. I hear the terrified screams of my baby brother Dani, who was only a few months old. He jumped and screamed, jumped and screamed with each volley. We spent days huddled together with our neighbors in a bomb shelter at the bottom of our building listening to the screams and cries of all the women and children each time a shell landed. I'm not exaggerating.

I felt badly for my mother raising three rambunctious boys: me, Sam; Wassim or Wess, who was a year and a half younger; and our little brother Dani, whom we thought, or at least I hoped, would be a girl because I'd always wanted a sister.

I was the worst of the three, hyperactive and always into some craziness. To give you an example, every time my dad would come home from flying all over the world, he would bring us toys from different countries and let me tell you, these were some cool toys. Within a couple of hours, I would have the hammer and screwdriver out taking them apart. Or, I'd climb to the fifth floor balcony and throw them off to see what good crash tests they could be. Once, my dad got me a nice, and I mean nice, 747 jetliner. The top half was clear so you could see the passengers and the stewardesses. But, being a kid growing up in Lebanon, I had to pretend to blow it up and then smash it with a hammer. Everyone tells me that I could have had a toy store by now.

Another time, when I was four and had just gotten picked up from kindergarten, I put on the paper hat I had made in class that day, walked up to the balcony on the fifth floor, went to the railing, dropped my pants, and proceeded to pee, yes, pee, all the way down five floors onto the people who were waiting at the bus stop. My dad saw me, ran to get his camera, took the perfect picture, and then beat my ass. Every time someone came over to visit, which was a lot in the Middle East, he would pull out the picture album and show it to everyone. There were also other pictures of me butt-naked, except for a holster holding two guns strapped around my waist. That was justified, you see, since I am a Texan by birth.

My days were action-packed. My mother had to tie me to the chair just to get a few dishes clean; she knew she couldn't turn her back on me just for a minute because if she did, it was trouble. I'm glad that all the buildings in Lebanon are made of concrete or I would have burned down our home a dozen times.

Before the war, there was no East or West Beirut. We could go to my grandmother's house in what later became East Beirut during the civil war. Before the war, my parents would drop my brother Wess and me there for the weekend. I was six at the time. Nana had two poodles that Wess and I loved to play with. We would ride on their backs and romp with them and never a growl would come out of them.

My grandfather and grandmother on my mother's side were Armenians. Their parents were slaughtered by the Turks. To this day, the Turks are not willing to admit that they killed a million Armenians with their swords, killing until the rivers ran red, even when the whole world knows it. My mother tells me that her grandparents in Armenia were wealthy and lived a good life before the Turks began their slaughter. My own grandparents met each other while on the run when they were forced to leave Armenia. They ran from country to country, eating grass to survive, and finally settled in Lebanon.

My grandfather was a mechanic who worked on large trucks. He and my grandmother were church-going people and, unlike me, never a bad word or a lie came out of their mouths. On Sundays, they would take us to church with them. We didn't understand much because it was in Armenian, but we didn't mind going either because there were a lot of kids our age to play with.

I forgot to mention that their home was next to the main water station in East Beirut, which became a major target during the civil war. A railroad track ran right by the house about thirty feet away. Wess and I always looked forward to seeing the train with its thick black smoke and loud steam engine going right by the house. Once, we tried to put rocks on the tracks to derail it. I know it sounds crazy, but if you knew me, you would understand. The train showed up right after we finished putting some big rocks on the rails and we ran like hell. We thought it would get the job done, but the train crushed the stones as if we'd only put grains of sand there. Now, of course, I'm glad that nothing happened because it would have been ugly.

My mischief kept my mom on her toes, but none of the chaos my brothers and I caused in those days could compare to what was ahead for us.

# Chapter 2
## 1975
## Civil War Erupts in Lebanon

The civil war broke out when I was seven. We could no longer go to my grandmother's because the section in which she lived became identified as East Beirut and we were in West Beirut, only ten minutes away. Big battles took place all around us. Of note was the battle over the famous Holiday Inn in Beirut.

It was the biggest and most luxurious hotel I had ever seen. Built of solid concrete and only two miles from our home, it had a casino, big underground theaters, and a rotating restaurant on the top floor. It also had elevators that ran up and down its exterior walls and was thirty floors tall, if not more. It became a battlefront and a strategic place in West Beirut; bullets and rockets were fired at it from every direction possible and it was burned several times, making it look like a beehive from inside and out.

I want you to imagine it. Every faction, including the Palestinians, tried to take over the hotel. In the hotel, the Christian militia fought to keep control, but every week someone claimed they had taken it away from them. There were a hundred militias in West Beirut and when some faction thought they had taken it over, they might get as far as the third floor. Then, the Christian militias, or the Phalangists, would come out of the underground theaters and take it back. Some factions even rolled cars loaded with explosives down the hill into the lobby. Even that did not bring it down.

Inside the Holiday Inn, the Phalangists set up dummies or decoys on tracks that moved back and forth just so they could see where the sniper fire came from. Finally, with the help of the PLO, the Muslim militias of West Beirut took it over.

I still remember the newspaper picture of a girl, a member of the Christian Phalangist militia, who wrapped herself in the flag of Lebanon and jumped to her death from the roof of the hotel rather than risk being captured by the Muslim militia. One man who was captured by them was killed, his body then dragged behind a station wagon all through West Beirut.

**Holiday Inn in Beirut damaged during civil war had not been restored as of August 3, 2010 when this photo was taken. All other bombed-out buildings had been restored or replaced.**

Things were so out of control and frightening, especially for kids. Even in the outdoor vegetable market, there were displays of jars containing pickled human body parts, such as ears, noses, hands, and even private parts. These were the result of torture from all sides.

Every night was the Fourth of July except it was real ammunition exploding in the sky, bursts of red, pink, orange, white, and green shooting in every direction. Wess and I would peek out the window when our mom wasn't looking. We saw the light show for a few moments until a shell landed nearby and our mother pulled us away from the window.

As things got worse - and by the way, I would never, ever use the expression "things couldn't get worse" because they always did in a big way - our government asked Syria to enter Lebanon to help stop the bloodshed. We had weapons sent to us from every place you can imagine: Russia, the U.S., Iraq, Saudi Arabia, Libya, and Iran. You name it; we had it.

The country became divided by what everyone called the Green Line which ran between East and West Beirut. I crossed the Green Line many times, but I will tell you of that later.

The Syrian army entered Beirut to help stop the civil war, but instead they made it worse because one day they would be on one side and the next day on another. They went back and forth like the high and low tides of the Mediterranean until they finally ended up siding with West Beirut, which was where I lived.

We missed a year from school because of the shelling back and forth and we couldn't see relatives in East Beirut and they couldn't see us. If you got caught on the wrong side, you might as well kiss your ass goodbye.

The Syrian Army surrounded East Beirut in 1978 and bombed it for two weeks. One morning, we got the awful news. I could tell that something was wrong when my mother, a very strong woman, started to cry while talking on the phone. I was surprised that the phone even rang, knowing how all utilities - power, water, and phone - hardly ever worked anymore.

My mother got off the phone and told us that Nana, our grandmother, had died in the shelling ten days ago. We were just now learning of it because the phones had been down. Because their house was next to the main water pumping station in East Beirut, it became part of a larger target. I was only ten and I could not believe that she was gone; even to this day I can't believe it. I'm sure from that day till this she has been my guardian angel.

They told us that my grandfather was okay, but that we needed to wait a few days to get him because of the intense fighting. My mother drove us over there to get my grandfather, who was still in shock. We drove through checkpoints and sniper alleys, where signs written with black markers warned "Drive fast - Snipers."

Most of the streets were destroyed and strewn with mangled debris. Burned cars that looked like empty shells were tossed all over the place. Finally, we arrived at what was supposed to be my grandparents' street, but it looked nothing like it; the water pumping station was hit badly, but not as badly as my grandmother's house.

You would think solid concrete would protect a little, but not when twenty rockets have slammed into it. Pieces of furniture were blown into the street and through the gap that was once the front of the house, you could see most of the downstairs and half of the upstairs. My grandfather was walking around in a daze, with tears in his eyes and looking as if he hadn't slept in weeks. My brother and I still couldn't believe that our grandmother was gone, so we started looking around under debris.

As we got into the house, we saw that the stairs going to the second floor lay in a big pile of rubble that someone had been digging through. As we walked closer to the small garden where my brother and I used to play, we were faced with a terrible smell and saw where the ground had sunk in the length of a person. My brother Wess turned to me and, as we looked at each other, my mother, my uncle, and my grandfather told us the indention in the ground was Nana's grave for the time being.

At ten years old, I asked a thousand questions. My mother said that my grandfather had buried her there because there were so many bodies to be buried that the hospitals and morgues could not handle any more and were going to start burning bodies. So, he decided to bury her.

After all the questions, I got the whole story. Apparently, when the Syrian Army started shelling, my grandmother was downstairs with her dog yelling up to my grandfather to come downstairs as the bombs got louder and closer. He could not hear her. A few seconds later, the house was hit with a barrage of rockets intended for the main water pumping station there in East Beirut, just twenty feet from their house. The stairwell collapsed on Nana and her dog. They both were killed instantly.

My grandfather, disoriented from the explosions, started to head downstairs and found out that the stairs were gone. It was a long way down, it was dark, and there was a lot of smoke. Some of the oil barrels he used for his work on trucks were on fire outside causing even more smoke.

Finally, after fumbling in the dark and calling for my grandmother not knowing where she was, he found his ladder. He climbed down while the shelling continued, calling her name. He went to a shelter two doors down to see if my Nana was there, but they were scared to open the door. So, he found himself wandering up and down the street looking for his wife.

After two days, the bombing subsided; he noticed an odor coming from the big pile of concrete that was once the staircase. He started digging with his bare hands until he uncovered her with her dog lying right beside her. He wrapped her badly crushed body in a sheet and, after finding out that they were burning bodies in the city, he found two men who dug him a shallow grave, keeping her there until things got better and she could be moved to a cemetery for a decent burial.

My brother and I were looking around to see if we could recognize anything in what was left of the home as we climbed over cinderblocks, glass, and rebar. We found our piggy bank, which Nana kept for us; it was still in good shape and had silver fifty-cent pieces and some paper money totaling around two hundred and fifty dollars, a lot of money back then.

My grandfather was able to find his money since he kept it all tied up in rubber bands and stashed several feet from the house. As my mother, my uncle, and my grandfather looked through the rubble, my brother Wess and I snuck up the ladder to see what remained of the upstairs.

The first thing we saw was the old clock that hung from the wall with a bird that came out every hour. We used to run to see it every time the clock rang. This time, it was on the ground and the glass that covered the face was broken. We tried to move the arms with our fingers to make the bird come out, but it was broken beyond repair.

There also was a fairly big painting of heaven and hell. Half of the painting showed nicely-dressed people with white dogs walking towards the bright light with angels. On the other side were burning buildings with drunks passed out on the streets, bottles of alcohol resting beside them. This all might sound weird, but there are some things that you see in your childhood that you never forget.

That night, after going home to West Beirut, our grandfather slept in the room with my brothers and me. We were so happy that he was with us. He prayed with us as he always did when we spent the weekends at his house.

A week or so passed by and finally they were able to move my grandmother to a cemetery. It was only a few of us there because of the war - my mother, her sister, my uncle and his wife, my grandfather, and the minister. As they were singing, Wess and I took the candles off all the other graves, set them down on her grave, and lit them. There were so many candles from so many graves that it looked like a bonfire.

A month later, things calmed down a little so we were able to send my grandfather to New York while the airport was still open. My aunt and my uncle had left Lebanon in the early seventies to live in Queens. They welcomed my grandfather into their home and took care of him. We were sad that he had to leave us, but we knew he had been through a lot. The poor man had to bury his own wife, not once, but twice; that's too much for anyone to go through.

# Chapter 3
## Militias, School, and Wild Dogs

And how had our country come to this? It is not a simple story, but the civil war I saw in the streets of Beirut was the result of friction between neighbors of different religious origins and political backgrounds along every street. Lebanon, just like Jordan, had to set up refugee camps for the Palestinians who overflowed into their countries when they were uprooted from their land and their homes in Palestine. The refugee camps were in southern Lebanon just across Israel's northern border, not far from the city of Beirut. Those camps, the most famous of which were Sabra and Shatila, were located only five miles from my home.

The people of Lebanon were Christian, Muslim, and Druze. Early on, the Christians were in the majority. Yasser Arafat, the leader of the PLO, was Muslim, and so the Lebanese Muslims and Druze welcomed him to Beirut and sympathized with the Palestinian cause. They also felt bolstered by the PLO guerrillas and hoped they could help them in their struggle for power against the Maronite Christians, who at the time were the majority in the Lebanese government.

Tensions escalated between the groups in the early 1970s because the PLO used southern Lebanon as a base for attacks against Israel, attacks which were met with harsh retaliation by Israel and that hit not only the Palestinians, but the country of Lebanon and its southern inhabitants.

Nevertheless, the Lebanese Muslims continued to look upon the PLO militia as comrades-in-arms, even though that alignment was drawing attacks from Israel on Lebanon. So, to combat this, the Lebanese Christians developed their own militias, such as the Phalangists and Tigers.

The government of Lebanon made up of Christians, Muslims, and Druze was in a chokehold and became ineffectual in calming the political and religious tensions within its borders. At one point, the Lebanese government even sought the help of Syria to quell the unrest spreading through Beirut in particular. Eventually, even the Lebanese Army became splintered into Christian and Muslim factions and it was difficult to tell which was which until a conflict erupted and each soldier sided with his own heritage, his own roots.

All of this became written in stone when in April of 1975 four Christian men in a church in East Beirut were shot and killed, two of them members of the Phalangist militia.

In retaliation, the Phalangists killed twenty-seven Palestinians as they rode through East Beirut in a bus.

The days of street fighting between Christian and Muslim militias began, starting a long and devastating civil war. And so, the city of Beirut was split in half with the East being predominately Christian and the West, Muslim.

The Green Line separating East and West Beirut was only two miles from our home. So, every time there would be fighting, you could hear it clearly. It was in the downtown area where all the banks, fancy restaurants, and hotels were and, as I mentioned before, the famous Holiday Inn. We often passed by the buildings while running errands with our parents in our white Volkswagen bug.

You could see the riddled buildings in the distance and burned floors with sandbags piled everywhere. I couldn't believe how many holes I saw: the little ones from small-arms fire to the bigger ones from the rocket-propelled grenades or RPGs to even bigger 155 mm Howitzer cannon shells. That was only what I could see from a distance. I was still young at the time. But later on, as I got older, I got a much closer look.

My brother and I attended a school overlooking Beirut International Airport from which my dad flew on a regular basis or whenever it was open. Eventually, we stopped going to that school because it was twenty minutes away and many times the bus driver would turn around and bring us back home because of the fighting, piles of tires burning in the middle of the road, or the automatic gunfire zipping past our bus. We were moved to private schools that were nearby so we could walk to school.

School was not my favorite place because the Lebanese schools were "old school." If you said the wrong thing or talked in class, the teacher would break out a wooden ruler, make you open your hand, and then hit you hard with it. If you moved your hand away while the ruler was in full swing, you would get an extra two whacks. In my case, being hyperactive, it meant a lot of those whackings. My grades were bad, and living in a war zone didn't help. I was more concerned about making it home from school in one piece.

Did I forget to mention the wild dogs that we would encounter in the streets on our walks to nearby schools? Some were missing legs and ears. Others foamed at the mouth while many bore bloody scars from fighting with other dogs or stains of oil from hiding under cars. Wess and I could have won the two hundred yard dash in the Olympics after having to run from those wild dogs.

There were days we couldn't outrun them, so we would jump on the roof of the nearest car until some older person with a stick would chase them away so we could come down. My poor brother had a complex. Every time he would see a dog, even when it was on a leash with its owner, he would jump on top of a car. I'm sure to him it wasn't funny, but to me it was a funny moment that never got old.

See, a lot of people during the war left in a big hurry and didn't take their pets with them. It was a life-or-death situation, so they let their dogs and cats run the streets of Beirut. No such thing as Animal Control, police, or even the fire department showing up for fear they would get shot as they had been shot at many times before. They wouldn't respond to anything. So, if your house was on fire or you got into an argument with your neighbor or even shot your neighbor, which happened a lot, no one would come. Life there was a do-it-yourself type of thing.

After my mother moved me from school to school, she found an American private school that only accepted American citizens, children of diplomats, or children of parents working with foreign embassies. In the fall of 1982, I started going to the American Community School or ACS. It was the nicest school I'd ever gone to and, if it wasn't for my mother, I would be running in the streets.

You see, my father, who wasn't involved in our schooling, would say that I should be working at a convenience store because there was no hope for me. I never forgot those words. My mother finally convinced him to pay my tuition, ten thousand dollars a year, a lot of money at the time.

At age fourteen, for the first time in my life, I was happy to go to school because they were nice to me there and helped me with my weak points instead of trying to beat them out of me. There were kids from all over the world and the teachers, mostly American, either lived on campus or a block away at the American University of Beirut, which was within walking distance of my house. It would take me ten minutes to go to school walking and twenty on the way back because it was downhill going and uphill coming back. There were long stairs between two apartment buildings and the Saudi Arabian Embassy next to our home. Those stairs and what happened there I will tell you about later.

My grades improved as the school year went by and the war seemed to subside a little with only a few explosions every now and then. People started to ignore the war and things seemed to get better. I even took music lessons and learned to play the saxophone, performing "The Pink Panther" for my parents at a parent-teacher meeting one night.

My brother Wess went to another school, The Lebanese International School, owned by Frank Reed, an American. While Wess was a student there, Mr. Reed was kidnapped by Lebanese Islamic militants, September 9, 1986, and held hostage for three and a half years, along with several other Americans and westerners who were kidnapped and held. Just another day in the turmoil that was Beirut, our home.

Both schools were good and were similar in their methods. I made a lot of friends and even had a beautiful Palestinian girlfriend named Zina. By the way, having a girlfriend meant only at school with a few kisses here and there. There was no "going out" or dating. You have to understand that in the Middle East most families don't let their daughters get out of sight unless they are engaged to be married.

As the school year got closer to the end, things got even better, although we still had a civil war and the Lebanese Army was still split in half between Muslim and Christian factions. At least we finally knew which side was which. Most of my friends in our neighborhood were a mix of religions: Muslims, Christians, and Druze, my father's religion. Because my mother was Baptist and always took us to her church, we did not learn our father's religion.

In spite of the different religions and economic levels of the kids in our neighborhood and at school, we were all good friends, got along well with one another, and enjoyed playing practical jokes on each other every chance we got.

**Sam at his desk at the American Community School or ACS located across from the American University of Beirut campus.**

# Chapter 4
## Summer Plans
### The Tennis Courts - The Soccer Field - The Syrian Army

Down the street from our house was the famous lighthouse of Ras Beirut. It was called Ras, which meant "head," because the land where the lighthouse sat jutted out into the sea. Before the war, the lighthouse was working. But when the civil war started, the light was turned off so it would not become an easy target.

The lighthouse was our hangout whenever things were quiet. Next to the lighthouse was a mechanic, a distant relative. We called him Mouallem, which is Arabic for teacher, because we used to watch him take engines apart and put them back together without a problem. If he did have a problem, he would sit back, light up a cigar for a few minutes, and the problem was solved. I looked up to him because he was teaching me.

My English was getting better from going to an all-English school. Just hearing it all day at school helped a lot, too. As the school year got closer to ending for the summer, my biology teacher asked me if I wanted to have the two hamsters that we had in our class. I was so excited because we never had pets in our house and, since I was getting the cage, the wheel, and the water bottle with it, I convinced my mother to let me bring them home.

Everyone was looking forward to the summer since the war had quieted down a little. Except for the skirmishes at the Green Line, stores were open and the electricity was on more than it used to be. The elevators were running in our building and we didn't have to walk up five flights of stairs, especially good after walking from school with our heavy book bags. You don't appreciate electricity until you lose it.

When my English teacher asked me what my plans were for the summer, I told her I'd go to the beach, play with my cousins, work at the tennis courts as a ball boy for some extra money, and make some new friends. At least, that is how I imagined my summer would be.

Even during the school year, when the weather was good on weekends, I would go to the tennis courts to hang out with my friends and make some money at the same time. And, since I was a little hyperactive, I was the best ball boy you have ever seen - skinny, but strong and fast. If the ball went over the wall, I would be over the wall and back with the ball in a split second. People that were members would wait for me to finish working one game so I could be their ball boy. They waited because they knew they would get all their balls back at the end of the game.

The family that ran the tennis courts were Lebanese Shiites or Shia Muslims who were forced to leave south Lebanon because of the war. Ahmed, his brother Muhammad, their little brother Mahmoud, and their dad were in charge. They taught tennis lessons and, when I wasn't chasing balls, I would watch them play. They were down-to-earth and treated me like family. At the end of the day, we would spray the courts with water and then brush over them with the welcome mat. Muhammad's dad always counted on me to clean the courts. No one liked doing it so they all seemed to disappear at the end of the day.

Muhammad and his family lived in what had been a small French fort during France's occupation of Lebanon. It overlooked the tennis courts, the soccer field, and the Mediterranean Sea. From the fort, you could really see how nice the tennis courts looked when we finished brushing them; it was amazing. The tennis courts were made of clay so they needed a lot of work on a daily basis. The lines had to be painted whenever they got worn. The clay was brushed by using a big, coarse welcome mat flipped over and attached by a rope to a two-by-four so it could be pulled behind you.

Being there gave me an escape from the war, a place to relax overlooking the sea, a place especially calming during sunset when the sun reflected off the water making it look like the sea was filled with little diamonds sparkling as the sun slid below the horizon. During the school year, I could see the Mediterranean from my school windows which helped me to daydream in math class since I didn't care for the subject or the teacher. She always smelled like alcohol and so did her coffee. But, living in a war zone could make anyone drink and smoke heavily, which a lot of people did. Most kids my age smoked but didn't drink much, even though there was no legal drinking age. We really didn't do it. You could send a six-year-old to any store with money and a piece of paper with "Johnny Walker" written on it and the store clerk would hand it over without question.

For the summer, I planned to work at the tennis courts just below the lighthouse. You have to remember that Lebanon is a small country and Beirut is a compact city. Adjacent to the tennis courts and the Mediterranean was a big soccer field where the Syrian Army had entrenched themselves in the red clay. On each of the field's four corners were big anti-aircraft guns with four barrels each. In the middle of the soccer field, there were little holes in the ground with metal plates shaped like an upside-down U where soldiers could sit protected and still be able to shoot out.

Everyone in Lebanon joked about the Syrians. Many came from remote villages in Syria and were not accustomed to things available in other countries. For example, they had checkpoints all over the city and, whenever they stopped your car, they would go to the back of the car and ask you to open the "trunk" even when the car was a Volkswagen like ours, which, of course, is where the engine is located. They would smile and then ask you to open the front. You had to keep a straight face because if you laughed at their ignorance of the anatomy of a Volkswagen, you would either be pistol-whipped, punched in the face, or taken away to fill sandbags for a day down by the Green Line, something I was made to do many times.

One morning on the way to school, I saw a Syrian officer and a soldier trying to open up the gas tank on a car. Apparently, the owner had put an extra lock on the tank to prevent his gasoline from being stolen. Since the Syrian army was in charge at the time, no one dared say a word.

As I got closer to the car, the soldier was getting frustrated because he couldn't get the tank open. He got so angry that he pulled out his gun to shoot the lock off and that's when the officer slapped him so hard that his gun fell out of his hand. I picked up my pace as I passed them while the officer was yelling at the soldier, calling him an idiot for almost blowing them both up.

At that point, I realized why the Syrian army couldn't take over East Beirut. They were not accustomed to house-to-house combat, which the Lebanese knew too well. But they were known for stealing any car they wanted in Beirut and in a few hours, it would end up in Damascus. No one in Beirut would dare confront them about the thefts or they would end up in the famous Syrian torture camps, which many Lebanese did and a few were lucky and lived to tell about it. The Syrians had so many intelligence agents and spies in Beirut that when we or anyone talked about Syria, it was referred to as "Switzerland" just as we referred to its inhabitants as the "Swiss."

The last week of school was fun especially when we turned in our books and got friends to sign our yearbooks. That was the first time I'd heard of a yearbook. It was all action shots, not the standard mug shots, which made it more fun. That was the only school I've ever liked and would look forward to going to each day, except for math class which by now I'm sure you've figured out wasn't my favorite. Most of the students who went to ACS lived on the American University of Beirut campus, a safe place at the time for Americans and foreign students. It was a beautiful place where Wess and I would often roller skate, something we looked forward to doing once school was out.

However, a summer of relaxation and fun was not to be.

**Sam and Ali working on the tennis courts.**

# Chapter 5
## June, 1982
## Israel Invades Lebanon

In June of 1982, on the last day of school, I was heading home with the hamster cage in my arms. The hamsters were standing on their back legs sniffing the air because it smelled different to them since we were outside and there was a lot of movement of cars and school buses, kids being picked up by parents, and cars honking.

You see, in Lebanon, honking is a language. Every second someone is honking whether it's traffic or just honking to be honking. In this Lebanese way of life, if you weren't shooting, you would be honking your car horn.

As I walked away from the school through a shortcut that I always took, things got quieter and the hamsters settled down. I got to the long stairs right near the Saudi Arabian Embassy. I was glad that my book bag was lighter with it being the last day of school. Carrying the hamster cage was hard enough going up those long, steep stairs between the Saudi Embassy and my home without having to carry a full, heavy book bag also. I was almost out of breath by the time I reached the top.

At the top of the stairs, I stopped to give myself a break and take a look at the hamsters when a barrage of anti-aircraft fire started to explode in the sky above me. After living in a war zone, you learned the difference between regular guns, artillery, mortar rounds, grenades, Kalashnikov AK-47s, M-16s, and a rocket-propelled grenade. This I already knew by the time I was just ten years of age.

The anti-aircraft firing continued as I rushed home. The shells shot up in the sky over my head and when they reached a certain altitude, they exploded.

As I started to walk faster, more anti-aircraft guns joined in. They were close and I knew they were coming from the soccer fields where they were set up on the field's four corners. My fast walk became a jog. I was only a block from the house when I heard jets, fighter jets, in the sky followed by more gunfire. It was loud and it never came to a stop.

The cars on our street were at a standstill with people honking nonstop because of the panic. Between the anti-aircraft fire and the honking and fighter jets streaming in the sky, I felt as if my heart rate went from ninety-eight to two hundred and twenty beats per minute in just one second. I was walking between cars which still were jammed in traffic. People were yelling at each other, their faces full of a fear I'd never seen before. That's when I knew something bad was going on.

A Palestinian fighter, taking advantage of the chaos caused by gunfire, walked up to a lady driving a nice Mercedes, grabbed her by her long blond hair, and pulled her out of her car through the window. You could tell from the look on her face that she was in shock. He saw an opportunity to own a nice new Mercedes and he took it.

I quickly got into the entrance of our building where I saw our neighbors and their kids with book bags all trying to squeeze into our five person elevator. Somehow I got in with everyone else and no one noticed the hamsters until one mom, trying to distract her child from what was happening, said "Look at what Sam has in the cage," which made everyone look.

Just for a moment, everyone was quiet until they got to their floors. When I got to our floor, our door was open and my mom rushed to me. The radio was on, and between the anti-aircraft gunfire, the radio, the honking of the cars, and jet fighters streaming through the sky, my brother yelled, "We are getting attacked by the Israelis!"

I ran to our bedroom, grabbed my binoculars, and asked my brother Wess where Dad was. My mom, carrying my little brother Dani who was screaming hysterically because of all the noise, said he had to leave for the airport because they wanted all the planes out of there before the airport shut down. Our neighbors across from us, who happened to be Palestinians, were talking to my mom and the whole building was trying to find out what was happening.

I ran to our back balcony, which had a concrete wall chest high, and saw the most amazing thing of my life: bullets and tracer rounds that lit up the sky. They were all going in the same direction, toward the Israeli jetfighters. And since the sun was close to setting, the colors were extremely bright.

I quickly adjusted the binoculars and followed the stream of automatic gunfire which led me straight to the jetfighters. They were dropping flares to avoid being hit by Russian-made, heat-seeking missiles called Sam-6.

My brother Wess was tugging on my arm, so I handed him the binoculars so he could take a look. Now you could see black smoke towering in the sky from a distance. At that point, I knew our summer was over. Our first color TV was tuned to the local news channel and they were announcing that the Israeli army was invading Lebanon. Minutes after the announcement, the power went out. We weren't surprised. After living in Beirut, we knew it was part of the war.

Our maid who lived with us was from Sri Lanka. Her name was Soma. She was shaking and in tears while trying to light up candles so we could see in the dark now that the sun was down. The streets were empty now; no more horns, no more traffic, only gunfire. Even the anti-aircraft fire had subsided since the jet fighters had finished their bombing runs. We had our transistor radios on; so did everyone on our street. That's all you could hear. Everyone had his own station on and it sounded like someone was on a loud speaker from a distance and you couldn't make out what they were saying. We could see the reflection of tracer rounds in the windows of the buildings across the street, and seconds later, the sound again of jetfighters. The Syrian and Palestinian positions opened fire with their anti-aircraft guns once again filling the sky with colors.

That night we didn't get much sleep. My mother spent the whole night filling every jar and bathtub with water because we knew that cutting off the water would be next.

Early in the morning, jets flew by and we heard huge explosions, big enough to rattle our building and the surrounding ones. A few minutes later, a broadcaster on the radio announced that the ammunition dumps were hit.

Usually ammunition dumps were in bomb shelters underneath buildings. This one, though, was under the big sports arena which was a mile from the airport. It contained so many rockets and so much ammunition that we heard continuous explosions for a solid week. A lot of civilians were hurt because the rockets would fly in all directions and land on top of buildings. No one would even dare get near the arena to put the fires out, because at any moment, it would start exploding again.

Within the first few days after the Israeli invasion, almost everyone in our building was gone. They gave us the keys so we could water the plants and keep an eye on things, and they were gone. Some made it to the airport just in time. Most of the others drove to Syria, and from there, to other countries.

To avoid boredom, Wess and I would go to different flats and leave candles burning in the windows to make the invaders believe that someone was living there. We also opened and closed the drapes daily to make it look as if the flat was occupied. We did this because many of the flats were being taken over by either refugees or Syrian military officials. One of the flats was in the building across the street from us, the same building where Max, our neighborhood dog, slept in the doorway. He also had to keep himself protected from the incoming Israeli gunboat fire which came daily.

One afternoon, as Wess and I were leaving one of the flats in that building having left a lighted candle in its window, Syrian foot soldiers met us in the main entrance. We heard Max starting to bark. There we were confronted by a senior Syrian officer with a sidearm and two soldiers following him with AK-47s and wearing combat fatigues.

The Syrian officer asked me who lived in that flat with the candle in the window. I lied and told him that it was our flat. He told me to hand over the key to the flat. I had a difficult time understanding him because his jaw had been wired shut.

After a few minutes of trying to understand what he was saying and with Max barking, my mom, who witnessed the whole thing from the fifth floor balcony of our building, flew down the stairs as fast as she could. No elevators working, of course.

She stormed across the street and got into his face and started to argue with him that we were not going to hand over the apartment to anyone. He started to get agitated and paced back and forth while other neighbors came out to see what the commotion was. At the same time that this was taking place, I kept trying to pet Max to calm him down, to keep him from getting shot. Finally, Max stopped barking, but he was alert, staying close to be protective of us.

After about fifteen minutes of my mother berating the officer, he said through his wired teeth, "You must be Christian!"

She stood tall, shoulders back, and said proudly that she was Christian and that her family had left Armenia to escape the murderous Turks. She said they had seen enough of his kind.

The Syrian officer had a puzzled look on his face as he and his two officers left the scene after getting no cooperation from my mother or the key to the flat.

# Chapter 6
## Hamster Therapy

Now there were only four or five tenants left in our ten-story building and no one to play with. We especially missed our next-door neighbors because there were four kids and we used to play Monopoly and Risk with them. Now it was only me, my brother Wess, and little Dani. The same thing started to happen all over the city. The people who didn't have the money needed in order to leave the city were forced to stay along with those like our family with a parent whose job required them to be there. All others fled. The only entertainment we had was the hamsters.

We handled the hamsters a lot so they were very friendly and never bit us. Within two weeks of having them, the mother had thirteen babies. We gave them lettuce and cucumber peels to eat even though hamsters are known to prefer sunflower seeds.

One day when I came home, I noticed that one of the baby hamsters was missing and that there was a pile of sawdust in the middle of the cage. When I looked outside the cage, I saw a Fisher-Price plastic hammer lying on the floor. When I uncovered the pile of sawdust, I found the missing baby hamster lying dead. Then I knew something was funny because hamsters never bury their dead and the hammer was next to the cage. The only one in the house that I could see committing this crime and then covering it up was my little brother Dani.

I called out to my mother who then called Dani, and when I showed her what happened, she looked at Dani, who was holding his finger and looking guilty. When I asked him why he did it, he said that the baby hamster bit him in the finger and so he smacked him on the head with the Fisher-Price hammer, not knowing it would kill him. He said he had given him a proper burial but I knew he covered him up hoping not to get caught. I could tell he was not only worried about getting caught, but also felt a little sick himself about what he had done.

When we played with the hamsters, we put them in toy cars and acted as if they were passengers or drivers which made time go by a lot faster during the war. One day my mom got tired of the hamsters because it wasn't long after that incident that more hamsters were born. I asked her to give me some time to find a solution.

One afternoon when there was a lull in the bombing, I ran down to my grandmother Teta's house to talk to my cousin Souheil because the phones weren't working and I couldn't call him. I found Souheil and I discussed the matter with him. He said to give him a few days and maybe we could build something for them. We found a great location on top of his house where there was a room that opened up to the roof where my uncle had grapevines, vines that were planted in the soil beside the building and grew up onto the rooftop over the fourth floor. There was also a rain barrel on the roof.

Souheil said to come back in a few days and he would have it ready. I told him I knew a carpenter that always threw away shavings, a good source of free bedding for the hamsters. Buying the shavings from the stores was expensive.

A few days later, he said that he was ready for the hamsters. I stopped at the carpenter's shop and got a tall bag of freshly-cut shavings. I carried the hamsters in the cage in one hand and the bag of shavings in the other. On the way there, everybody stopped to look at the hamsters and ask me what they were.

Once I got to Souheil's house, he was very excited to show me what he had come up with for the hamsters, a huge L-shaped aquarium. We poured all the fresh shavings in first and then the hamsters. They looked like they were on vacation in their spacious new home. We threw in empty toilet paper rolls and the hamster wheel, which later broke when fifteen hamsters tried to sleep in it all at the same time. We decided not to buy any more toys for them since they were expensive. Also, we didn't want to take a chance on going all the way to the pet store which might not even be open because of the war. We decided to put the pregnant hamsters in the carry cage when we discovered that the males would eat the newborns.

We would make it a business. My cousin bought one brown hamster - mine were all white - and that way all the new breeds came out with different shades of brown and different color eyes.

Playing with the hamsters was our great escape from the war. After a few months, we had about fifty or sixty hamsters and we started selling them to the pet store for five dollars apiece. My cousin came up with the idea that we should even grow our own sunflower seeds to save on the cost of food.

We were doing well with the hamster sales and we were finally able to sell the grandmother of all the hamsters to the pet store owner even though he had been snatching her out of the batch we were offering to sell him, setting her aside because she was old and had a bald spot on the top of her head. After a few tries, we were finally able to sell her to him. We couldn't believe how long she had lived.

One day I decided to be a physical therapist to one of the female hamsters that was pregnant because I noticed that she was not leaving her nesting spot. When I picked her up, my cousin and I saw that there was a string tied around her waist from one of the cut-up rags we had thrown into the cage. Since the string had been tied around her waist for such a long time, her lower body was paralyzed. After removing the string, I tried to massage her back and manipulate her spine back and forth when I heard a pop. She stopped moving. She was dead. We were very upset and decided not to put any more stringy rags in the cage so it wouldn't happen again.

We were doing well with the selling of the hamsters until the civil war intensified between East and West Beirut and the shelling resumed. The stores all shut down again and we could not even give the hamsters away, leaving us with two hundred and fifty of them. My cousin and I decided to separate all the males from the females so there would be no more babies. It got so frustrating that we wondered if putting Souheil's cat in the cage might help solve our problem.

Souheil's cat was different than any other cat you have ever seen. He was very big, gray, with stripes like a tiger, and had six toes on each paw. He was a nice cat, but looked intimidating if you didn't know him. We decided to put him in the cage.

We opened up the lid and gently sat him inside. All the hamsters stood up on their hind legs and started sniffing him. They did not seem a bit scared of him. He, on the other hand, immediately wanted out of the cage and wanted to have nothing to do with the hamsters. We were shocked that this big cat seemed intimidated by the little hamsters. We laughed at him and then decided to see if the hamsters could swim.

As an experiment, we put them in the rain barrel, starting with just five, and they immediately started swimming in circles. So I said to my cousin, "Let's wash all the hamsters."

We would put five in at a time, take them out, and dry them with a towel since we couldn't use a hair dryer because, of course, there was no electricity. It took us about two hours to wash all the hamsters and put them back in their cage. They all had that fuzzy look and were grooming themselves, rubbing their front paws alongside their noses.

To top it off, we decided to spray them with Drakkar Noir cologne, which was very expensive cologne in the eighties. They all smelled great, but they kept rubbing their noses because it was not their scent. Now we were the only hamster owners in Lebanon that had not only the cleanest cages, but also the best smelling hamsters.

By then, the sunflowers we had planted were fully grown. Without our knowing it, one of my uncles had sprayed our sunflowers with pesticides, thinking he was helping. My cousin harvested the seeds from the sunflowers and fed them to the hamsters. Of course, it wasn't until later when our uncle told us he had sprayed the flowers with a pesticide that we realized why most of the hamsters died.

That was the end of our hamster business. I still miss them to this day because I learned so much from them. They were a big part in helping me cope with the war and all that was going on around me.

# Chapter 7
## Gardening, Science Experiments, and My Grandmother's Bunker

All my cousins and my grandmother from my dad's side of the family lived on the other side of the lighthouse, which is also a ten minute walk from our house. They had a better view of the Mediterranean there. They lived on ten acres with four buildings where my uncles, my dad's brothers, all lived with their families. In the middle was a huge garden that my father and uncles planted during the war so we could have vegetables, and a chicken coop for fresh eggs. Not only did they grow vegetables, but also fruit: peaches, grapes, bananas, plums, even papayas that my dad flew in with him from the Philippines and two tall palm trees that were planted many years ago by my grandfather. He passed away when I was five and left the land and the buildings to my uncles.

My dad and my uncles all had green thumbs, so no matter what they planted, it grew like you have never seen before. The only two things my dad knew how to do were fly a 747 jumbo jet and garden.

And speaking of gardening, one day four of us, my cousin, two neighborhood kids and I, found an unexploded anti-aircraft shell that looked like a bullet on steroids in my uncle's garden. The top of the bullet was circled with black, green, and red lines which meant that it was a tracer round that would either explode at a designated altitude or when it came in contact with its target. We knew there would be a lot of gun powder in it and we didn't have any pliers big enough to be able to twist off the top to get the gun powder. We also didn't know if that would be safe because trying to twist off the top might cause it to explode.

We decided instead to take it out of sight behind my Uncle Hussein's house. We got a hacksaw and a bottle of water. Before we started sawing, we looked at the back of the casing to see if the firing pin had been ignited. It showed that the bullet had been used and was a dud, making it even more dangerous.

One of the boys suggested that while somebody used the hacksaw on the bullet, someone else would pour water to keep it from sparking. We had just started sawing the bullet, only getting about a quarter of the way down, when I felt a flashing sting spread across my back which made me jump like Michael Jordan. Uncle Hussein had seen us and had picked up a young, green bamboo stick which made a whooshing noise as he swung it across my back. He was cussing and swinging the bamboo at the same time while I was running around trying to recover from what felt like a thousand bee stings.

"Are you trying to kill yourselves?" he asked.

All the other kids got a taste of the bamboo stick, but mine was the worst because unlike them, I was not a moving target. In all this commotion and pain, I managed to grab the anti-aircraft shell and the hacksaw and run as fast as I could as tears ran down my face from the pain, but I kept thinking how much fun we were going to have once we got this shell open since it had more gunpowder than any of us had ever seen.

We ran down to a small open field out of Uncle Hussein's view, a field across from the sea that was used by Palestinians firing back at Israeli gunboats. We began sawing the bullet again and once we got halfway through, we started to feel greater resistance, but we kept sawing.

Once the task was complete, we looked inside and could see an igniting rod that was full of holes so that there was a faster rate of ignition which sent the bullet skyward at a faster rate. An ordinary bullet ignited from a small cap at its base. Discovering this was like being in science class doing our own science experiment. Our science teacher would have been proud that we used water to cool the metal preventing any sparks. If it had ignited, there would have been the end of all four of us.

We were able to get between three and four cups of high-grade gunpowder from the shell and gave it a day to dry in the hot Mediterranean sun. We found an anthill containing large ants next to a large fig tree on my grandmother's property. That would be our target, the anthill.

We took straws connecting them together end to end and then inserted them into the anthill. We began pouring gunpowder down the straws, slowly filling the anthill and causing the ants to become very agitated, swarming around the anthill and trying to crawl all over us.

Once the anthill was filled to the top, we quickly made a line of gunpowder across the ground away from the ants giving us distance both from the biting ants and the impending explosion. Once we were all clear, a few more kids ran over to see what all the excitement was about. They were amazed at how much gunpowder we had.

We looked around to make sure Uncle Hussein was not around as one of our friends, who was a smoker at thirteen, lit a match to the line of gunpowder on the ground. To our surprise, the fire ran the line more quickly than we could have imagined. It was at lightning speed. It seemed that as soon as his match touched the gunpowder, it had already reached its destination. It made a whooshing noise for only five seconds and we could see a light green which changed to white hot emitting from the anthill as if it were a jet engine.

The fire was out within seconds and then white smoke emerged not only from the anthill but from other holes around that area connected to the anthill that we did not know about. Only a few half-burnt ants close to the top survived, but thousands were instantly fried.

Everyone was shocked to see how powerful the two cups of anti-aircraft gunpowder were. Another afternoon of entertainment for Beirut survivors was over and no one got killed except a colony of ants.

\* \* \*

My brother and I went to my grandmother Teta's a lot because we were close to our cousins. The ground floor of Teta's house was used as a bomb shelter. When my grandfather dug the foundation, he hit solid rock three feet thick making it perfect for a bomb shelter.

In the beginning days of the invasion, my brother and I went there to get some vegetables for my mom so she could make us the best Lebanese food you have ever had. We saw all my uncles and cousins filling up sandbags. We quickly joined them and started to help barricade the windows on the ground floor, the safest spot there with its three feet of solid rock.

At the age of fourteen, this was all so exciting. Now we had a good excuse to tell my mom that it was safer there than at our house. If we went there and the bombs started to fall, she didn't have to worry.

Also, there was an old well that had been hand-dug by my grandfather and his cousin that was later reopened. They hooked up a pulley and a bucket to bring the water up. I couldn't believe that it was dug by hand. When I took a look down the well while Uncle Hussein grabbed me by the waist, I was shocked at what a long, long way it was to the bottom and thankful my uncle didn't lose his grip or try to teach me another lesson!

Now my grandmother's house was pretty much a bunker. Teta was deaf, but if you yelled in her ear, she could hear you, and when bombs fell near, she could feel and hear them.

In the streets of Beirut, every pickup truck was outfitted with an anti-aircraft gun or a fifty-caliber machine gun. They would drive in the streets firing at the Israeli jets and sometimes, from being in such a hurry, they would hit the tall buildings by accident if or when a fighter jet flew behind it. Now you have to worry about getting shot by both sides in the invasion. But at Teta's, in her bunker, we felt safe.

# Chapter 8
## Max, Roaches, and Burning Trash Piles

The only time it got quiet was at night, and then it was the wild dogs running the streets, one of which was Max. He stayed right outside my friend Omar's house, across the street. Omar and his family fed him whenever they had leftovers. He looked out for the neighborhood and wagged his tail when he saw us playing soccer in the street. He was dirty and I don't think he was ever given a bath, but he was the neighborhood dog. Whenever other dogs would wander into our street, he would quickly approach them and they would cower before him. If he didn't like them, he would make them leave with a growl that would scare the crap out of anyone. Max knew all the kids on our street and most of them were refugees from other parts of Lebanon. If we walked anywhere, he would follow us around like a chaperone at a party.

We would go down the street to talk to the Palestinian fighters, whose positions were set up fifty feet from the lighthouse, giving them a good view of the shoreline. From there you could see the Syrian Army dug in at the soccer fields. We couldn't even go to the sea anymore because they had mined the beach road and, in some places, you could see wires leading to the rocky beach meaning big explosives were rigged in case the Israelis tried to come from the sea.

It started to get very boring because we could only venture out within the one-mile radius of home and so, with no TV and nothing to do but play cards and drive my mother crazy, we decided to take care of the trash problem on our street.

There was an enormous trash pile at the corner of our building where everyone threw their trash, and with no trash pickup, dogs, cats, and let's not forget our healthy Lebanese rats, tore through the bags making a bigger mess. Roaches were everywhere and to tell you how big they were you would think I was exaggerating. They could fly, and I don't mean just two feet off the ground, all the way to the fifth floor. Let me tell you how I found out.

One night we were trying to get some sleep. All our windows were open because it was so hot during the summers in Lebanon and no electricity meant no air conditioning. So, we just lay there sweating in the heat without any breeze, which made it worse. Most of the time, my brothers and I would sleep with our pants on, and sometimes our shoes, in case something happened in the middle of the night we could be ready to run to the bomb shelter quickly.

That night, I was almost falling to sleep when I felt something crawling on my back. Being half asleep, I didn't realize what it was until it got between my shoulder blades. That's when I felt its antennae brushing my neck. It made every hair on my body stand up and gave me chills even though it was a hundred degrees in our bedroom.

Still lying on my stomach, I quickly reached over with my left hand and scrapped it off me. I jumped to my feet with my flashlight in hand, the one I always kept by the side of my bed. I shined the light on our carpet and there it was: the mother of all roaches. I stomped it with my shoe that I was sleeping in until you could barely see it and then a few more times because it scared the shit out of me. Now there was no way I could go back to sleep after what had just happened. I spent the rest of the night scanning the corners, the walls, and the ceilings of our bedroom with my flashlight.

The next morning, I ran down the street to tell my friends that from now on we were going to burn the trash. I passed by the Palestinian fighters who hid their jeeps underneath the building to avoid being seen by Israeli jets in the daylight. The jeep had a 106 mm gun on it.

The Palestinian soldiers were always nice to us and offered us some of their food whenever they had any. When one of them overheard me talking about burning the trash, he came up to me and said I would need gasoline, which in those days was hard to find. We started to look at cars in the streets that were left behind with no owner around. We opened the gas tank on one and put a small gauge hose all the way down inside. We got a little gas which filled up two small bottles, but we needed more.

The fighter told us all to sit on the trunk, and, with about eight kids on the back of it, the car sank down allowing the rest of the gas to roll toward the hose. We learned something new that evening.

We dumped the gasoline all over the pile of trash, and, because the pile was huge, we had to climb over the nasty bags of garbage to start the fire. Luckily, my mother didn't see us or she would have gone nuts. She made us take showers every night no matter how many bombs were landing on us.

I lit the fire and within seconds it was a big one. Suddenly things started to explode - aerosol cans and other things. You could also see the roaches trying to escape by the hundreds, but not in time. The flames got higher and higher when we suddenly realized that the city's phone box was mounted on the wall right behind the fire. It started to turn red from the heat. We laughed about it because the phones never worked anyway, so no one cared.

My brother Wess wanted to make things more entertaining, so he threw a box of AK-47 bullets into the fire. There were thirty rounds in each box. We all looked at each other and then started running. In a few minutes, everyone who had been on the balconies watching the big blaze ran for cover, the bullets starting to explode in all directions.

When my mother asked Wess and me what we had done, we both said there must have been something in the trash.

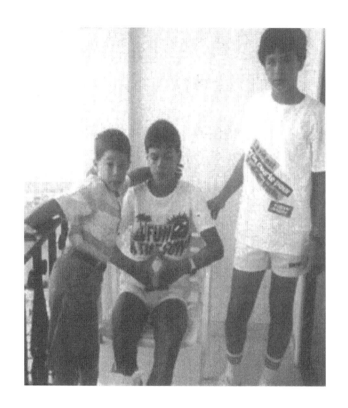

**Dani, Sam, and Wess on the balcony.**

# Chapter 9
## Flares, Refugees, and a Few Broken Eggs

At sunset things were quiet and we did the same nightly routine: light up candles and kerosene lanterns that were very bright which helped us play cards. Of course, my brother and I would fight because one of us would get caught cheating and the fists would start flying.

After the cards, my mother would heat up water on the gas stove; then we would take the hot water and dump it in a big plastic container adding just enough cold water from the bath tub to make it a desirable temperature. I would stand on the tile bathroom floor and using a smaller can, scoop out the water and pour it over myself. Then it would be my brother's turn

One night, the Israeli jets started to drop flares and what a sight it was! The flares fell in the formation of a crescent and because it was a hot summer night with no breeze, the flares came down even more slowly.

As soon as the flares started to come down, everyone began shooting at them, especially with tracer rounds used to show where the bullets are going. We would watch and cheer and when they hit the target, everyone would yell as if it were a soccer game. This happened for a few days until it was announced on the radio not to shoot at the flares because the jets could see where the bullets were coming from and could make it a target during the day.

With the Israeli army moving also through southern Lebanon, even more refugees came to Beirut. It was a big rush into the city. People would just go into any building and move into any vacant apartment. No rent, no nothing. Even farm animals were brought into buildings which was the funniest thing I have ever seen. You would see chickens running around on balconies and goats on roof tops.

In one incident, the owner of a very nice building with its own generator behind Grandma Teta's house came to check on his building because he heard that refugees were moving in. As he got to the entrance, he saw two people trying to get a cow in the elevator so they could take it upstairs. He had a heart attack and died right there.

The more the Israelis pushed north from southern Lebanon, the more the refugees moved into West Beirut. People got into shoot-outs over who was taking over an apartment and which floor belonged to whom, and with no law enforcement whatsoever, it was chaos.

This is how much worse it got. One day Wess and I went out with our little brother Dani. Normally, we didn't like taking him with us because we didn't want anything bad to happen to him. He was only six years old and was crying because we were going to leave him at home again. We decided to take him with us to our grandmother's so we could play with our cousins. But before we could even leave the house, Dani was on the balcony pointing to a building next to the Saudi Arabian Embassy. He asked if we could stop there for a minute to say "hi" to a friend of his whom he could see waving to us from a window on the back side of the third or fourth floor facing a parking lot. We ran over there and from the parking lot, they said hello to each other while Wess and I admired the Saudi Arabian Embassy with its nice palm trees, beautiful landscaping, and cute girls playing soccer there. We were only there a few minutes when Dani said he was done saying hello. So, we continued our walk to Teta's.

When we got there, one of my uncles who did most of the gardening when my dad wasn't there, called me over to give me some fresh vegetables and fresh eggs to take home with me. I had just set the basket of vegetables and eggs down so we could play some soccer with my cousins when we heard an explosion in the distance; we knew it couldn't have been jets bombing because we didn't hear them nor did we hear any anti-aircraft fire.

Suddenly, everyone was pointing in the direction of the building where we lived. I ran up the street to get a better look and I could see a mushroom cloud in the distance followed by black smoke. I grabbed my little brother's arm and the basket of vegetables and eggs and started to run in the direction of our building.

Right in front of us was Wess, who was able to run faster because he wasn't carrying anything. The closer we got to our street, the faster my heart raced. I felt as if I had tunnel vision, my eyes fixed on the smoke cloud, when I realized it wasn't our building even though from a distance it looked as if it were. I had a feeling of relief, but was still afraid.

As I got closer to the entrance of our building, I could see the devastation right by the Saudi Arabian Embassy. It was the building that we were standing underneath just thirty minutes ago with my little brother Dani saying hello to his friend. The building was sheared in half and you could see furniture and bedrooms still intact as if someone had taken a knife to a cake and cut away half of it without disturbing the other half.

We ran up the stairs as fast as we could, out of breath by the time we got to our floor. We began banging on the door for my mother to open up. I looked down to check on the eggs in the basket and noticed that some were broken in the bottom. It didn't bother me because at least we had a building to go to, one that was still standing. A few broken eggs were the least of my worries.

Finally the door opened and when I saw my mom's ashen face, I knew she was scared although she tried to play it off so we wouldn't be affected by it. As the three of us hurriedly pushed our way in, we saw our maid Soma in the kitchen crying. They were a lot closer to the explosion than we were and they could see the fractured building from our balcony clearly.

I set the basket with the eggs and vegetables in the kitchen and ran to our balcony to see the building where we were thirty minutes ago. It had been blown in half and the guards from the Saudi Arabian Embassy were shooting in the air to let the ambulance know where to come. In the language of the Lebanese during war, if you can't see the smoke, follow the gunfire and you will find it.

On the balcony, my brother Wess was saying to my mom that we were just there to see little Dani's friend. As he spoke, you could hear the sirens getting closer and people rushing to the scene. We asked my mom if we could go there to get a better look, but she wouldn't let us.

Disappointed, we walked back to the balcony. When we got there, we could hear a woman screaming and beating her chest with her fists. She was wearing a scarf on her head, covering her hair, and was crying hysterically. Just hearing her scream and beat her chest was so sad that I'm thankful my mother didn't let us go.

The whole street was quiet now but for her screams. I waved at my friend Omar and his family, who were on the first floor in the building across from us doing the same thing we were. Even Max, our neighborhood dog, was standing with his ears perked in the direction of the ambulance.

A fire truck showed up also, which was a surprise because in Beirut no one shows up. We waited anxiously to hear of survivors. We heard on the radio that there were survivors on one half of the building and they were still digging for the rest.

It started to get dark and because we couldn't see what was going on, we went back inside to do what we did every night: light all the candles and fill up my favorite kerosene lamp. Even in the midst of unimaginable tragedy and the ongoing threat of even more, we tried to maintain a daily routine which included lighting up the night in the only way we could.

You could tell who in the city had the kerosene pressure lamps because of their distinctive brightness. The lamps were chrome and had a knob which you pulled out, pumping in air to build up pressure to light the lamp. It had such an intense brightness that you couldn't look at it as you lit it unless you wanted to be blind for the rest of the night.

That night we found out from one of the surviving neighbors in the building that blew up that a little boy and his mother died, but the boy's father and brother survived because they were on the opposite end of the house at the time of the blast.

And the reason for the explosion? An argument between two families over an apartment. Someone detonated a bomb killing all those innocent people.

That night, as I lay in bed thinking about what had happened and how close we were to dying, I asked myself why God would let a boy and his mother die while letting the dad and another son live. How that father must have felt surviving when his wife and boy died, I could not imagine.

**Apartment building pancaked by explosions sits amid buildings as yet untouched.**

# Chapter 10
## Finally, a Peaceful Sleep

During the night, I was awakened by a mosquito buzzing in my ear. I jumped up and saw that my brother Wess had a shoe in one hand and a flashlight in the other. Every time a mosquito would land on the wall, he would smack it so hard that it would end up as flat as the wall it landed on.

My little brother slept in between us, three beds pushed together, with Wess closer to the big glass sliding door, Dani in the middle, and me on the other side. I joined in on killing the mosquitoes, but the more we killed, the more showed up. They were all coming from the balcony, but it was too hot to close the sliding glass doors.

We were both surprised that our little brother was still snoring despite our mosquito patrol. We finally gave up swatting them against the wall because the wall was now marked with patterns of blood when we made contact or the imprint of a dirty shoe when we didn't. Also, our batteries started to run low.

We lit a candle and I told Wess to go to the kitchen to get the Katols, green mosquito repellant coils. You lit the outer end of it and it burned slowly from outer tip end, around and around the coil to the inside tip end, and gave out a smell that mosquitoes didn't like.

He was scared to go and so was I because it was dark and we could hear gunfire and what sounded like artillery fire in the distance. So we decided to go together with a candle in one hand and a blanket in the other, not that we used the blankets in the hot summers of Lebanon, but it felt safe to hide underneath them.

As we walked down the hallway towards the kitchen, we could see our shadows walking with us making it even scarier. We finally made it to the kitchen. I set the candle, glued by candle wax onto a small tea saucer, on the kitchen counter. My brother started to open up the drawers slowly so we would not make any noise when, out of the corner of my eye, I saw something white next to us.

I quickly grabbed the candle and turned as fast as I could to see what the hell it was and to our surprise, it was our maid, Soma, smiling at us in the dark. I was so startled that I didn't feel the hot wax that had dripped on my hand until it was completely dry.

After Wess and I finally got our heart rates back to normal, we both said, "What are you doing in here?"

She smiled again with her bright white teeth that scared us in the pitch black darkness, her dark skin making them appear even brighter. She said she was getting some water. She turned around giggling knowing how badly she just scared us and went to her little room, a room where we also stored all our canned food.

Wess and I returned to our room and lit five of the Katol coils; we figured if one was good, five would be even better. We lit them and put them all around the beds. Then we thought that if we closed the sliding glass door for a little while, the smoke could build up, and the mosquitoes would not have a chance of surviving. Within fifteen minutes, our room looked like someone had thrown a smoke grenade into it.

And I'm sure breathing all that stuff wasn't the best thing for us. I decided to open the glass sliding door and slowly the smoke started to roll out like fog lifting over a pond. I stepped outside onto our balcony and waited for the smoke to clear.

Looking down from the fifth floor, I had a good view of the trash pile and it looked as if it had grown overnight. I could hear the tinkering of cans and an occasional "meow."

Then in the moonlight, I saw some big rats walking along the wall leading to the trash and when they got to the first bag, they all stood on their hind legs and started to sniff the air. The amazing thing was that the cats were only a couple of feet away tearing their own bags of trash and paying no attention to the rats. It was as if the cats knew that either the rats were too big for them or they were all trying to survive and there was enough trash for everyone.

I asked Wess to hand me a tennis ball so I could throw it towards the trash pile to scare the rats and the cats, when I turned around and realized that Wess was in his bed already asleep. I was talking to myself.

That night was quiet except for the occasional coughing and hacking from the refugees across the street. As I lay in my bed, I couldn't believe how much more you could hear when there is no electricity, how the sound of air conditioners and refrigerators, elevators and fans, really muffled all the sounds that we heard at night. And that night we finally slept peacefully in the quiet, warm air without bugs, roaches, or mosquitoes buzzing over our heads.

But of course, we should have known it was just the calm before the storm.

# Chapter 11
## Psychological Warfare

It was just before dawn when two loud roars followed by two big booms shook the buildings and shattered glass. Then screams and anti-aircraft fire followed. It happened so fast that I went from a dead sleep to grabbing my little brother Dani and putting him against me as a protective shield while a big thump came from the other side of the bed.

We could hear screams and yelling from our street followed by much profanity. Our hearts were pounding when my mother ran into our room asking if we were okay. I realized that I was using my little brother as a shield and, from the look on his face, he knew it too. It took us a few seconds to realize what had happened and with a whisper I said to him, "Sorry. I didn't mean to do that. I was scared."

My brother Wess got back up from behind his bed with his pillow in both hands pressed against his chest. He was right by the glass sliding doors, the worst place to be if they were shattered by gunfire or explosions. After everyone calmed down, Soma yelled from the kitchen, fear in her voice, "Madam, is everybody all right?"

My mother told us it was jets flying at a very low level. They must have bombed the soccer fields where the Syrian army was because it sounded so close. Before she left the room to check on Soma, she told us to stay away from the glass. As she turned around, Wess and I looked at each other as if saying "You must be crazy. If that glass door shattered, there would be no way to avoid it falling on all three of us."

Now there was no way we could go back to sleep; being scared to death caused an adrenalin rush in both of us. Wess and I got some masking tape and started to tape up the glass sliding door just as we had seen everyone who grew up in the war do. As we put tape across the glass to keep it from falling and causing severe injuries, we could hear the sound of glass being scooped up with dust pans and brooms from balconies across the street.

In the midst of taping the glass, we heard a "psst, psst" coming from the first floor apartment over the coffee shop. We couldn't see that well because the sun was just starting to come up behind our building. Then we saw that it was Omar and we waved back.

Wess, trying to keep a low voice, said, "Where did they hit, where did they hit?" and Omar yelled back knowing that everyone is awake now, "It was only a sonic boom."

We had heard sonic booms since I was a child, but never one as loud and window chattering as this one. Apparently they had flown over us at a very low altitude which is why it was so loud and destructive. It was a kind of psychological warfare designed to scare and disturb the enemy and disrupt daily life. That was also their reason for cutting off the water and electricity, but they forgot that the Lebanese people were and had been used to interruptions in utility services way before the Israeli invasion.

Omar yelled at us again and said he would talk to us later because his parents didn't want him to stand outside on the balcony after what had just happened. Wess and I went back into our room.

Sitting there, I thought about the hamsters which helped keep us sane during all this craziness and wished we still had them. I remembered how they would stand on their back legs sniffing the air. If I opened the door of the cage and put my hand in, they would climb into my hand as if they couldn't wait to see me. They had been our constant companions and a source of comfort in times like these. If nothing else, I could keep the memory of them and the peace they gave us.

# Chapter 12
## An Average Day:
## Water Runs, Israeli Bombs, Soccer Games, and AK-47s

The tennis courts became off limits since the Syrian forces were hunkered down in and around the soccer field. We started to drive my mother insane, pleading with her to let us play in the street for a little while. Sometimes she would say "yes," but most of the time it was "no," and lots of times she had to break out my dad's belt and threaten the both of us, Wess and me, to keep us from killing each other!

About nine o'clock one morning after the sonic boom scare, someone told my mother that the drinking water was on. But, it couldn't be pumped up to the water tank that sat on top of the building and fed all the pipes because there was no electricity.

So, we got all our buckets and big plastic twenty-five gallon containers, which everyone who lived in Beirut owned for hauling either water or gasoline. My brother and I felt we were responsible for keeping water in our bathtub, in all the containers, and in the toilets. We would race down the stairs with the plastic containers banging against us, occasionally falling on top of each other with a bunch of loud booms, the sound of empty containers hitting the ground.

It didn't matter how much noise we made because our building was pretty empty except for our floor, the eighth floor, where the Syrian owner of the building lived and where a French lady lived with her cat, and the ground floor, where the concierge of the building lived with his wife and children. In order to get to the water, we had to walk by his small flat and through a little courtyard and wait in line to fill up our containers.

Sometimes there would be Palestinian fighters from the surrounding buildings doing the same thing. We would let them go in front of us so we could spend more time out of our flat while also getting a closer look at their weapons, which they were glad to display for us. On some occasions, they let us carry them while they filled up their water jugs and metal canteens.

That water spigot was like a watering hole in the middle of the desert bringing us all closer together. It didn't matter if you came from a rich family or a poor one, during the invasion, we were all one and we all suffered together. There was no discrimination. We looked up to the Palestinian soldiers because they were fighting for their homeland and in a way, we felt we were fighting with them.

After many trips up and down, to and from the fifth floor, my brother and I had a system going. As I was on my way up with two full plastic gallon jugs with the occasional stop for a rest, Wess was on his way down with two empty ones. We had to be quick about it because we never knew when the water was going to be shut off by the water company. The water was on sporadically when it came on and then it was on for only a few hours.

But this day we had enough time to even fill my mother's plant sprayers, which looked like water guns and were also entertainment for us. We would go to our back balcony, which had a reinforced concrete wall that came to our necks. We would then pull out a couple of stools so we could get a better view of the sky and the buildings around us. Looking out we could see the mosque's tall tower with speakers used five times a day to call people to prayer. Right across the street from its tower was a church with a smaller bell tower which rang every Sunday morning.

Wess and I would pump up the spray guns by pulling up and down on a lever to force in air enabling it to shoot a fifteen foot stream into the air. When the Israeli jets flew over our building being chased by the colorful anti-aircraft fire, we shot our plant sprayers at them, pretending that we, too, were shooting anti-aircraft bullets at them. Like clockwork, the Israeli jets would fly over our building around three in the afternoon and drop their bombs. Our water guns were always ready for action.

A month into the invasion, the Israeli military was on the outskirts of the city and now the bombs fell harder than ever. They not only fell from the air, but also came across land and from the sea. The Israeli Navy started shelling us non-stop without discrimination. No one could drive on the roads close to the beach and all the roads leading to the beach had huge piles of dirt and rocks at the end of them to block the view of our streets from the Israeli gunboats.

Our introduction to the gunboats came one day when we begged my mother to let us play in our street just for a little while and, to our surprise, she said "yes" even though she had just returned home with a bag full of puzzles and European comic books like Asterix, Obelix, and Tin Tin to keep us occupied. Puzzles and comic books saved our sanity and helped us escape the hell hole we were enduring.

When we heard the word "yes" from my mother, we ran through the door at full speed like convicts escaping from death row. We ran down the long stairs jumping over the last few steps. Within seconds, we were on the ground floor. We dashed out the gray gate of our building into the street yelling our friends' names like animals on a stampede.

All the kids who were left on our street were refugees from different parts of the country and although they were poor, they always had smiles on their faces when they saw us coming down the street. We greeted each other with hugs and kisses as if we hadn't seen each other in years. War made all equal in Beirut.

Within a few minutes, a few more kids showed up with a soccer ball which was stuffed with newspaper because it had a hole in it. A few weeks before, we had been playing when shells started to land everywhere and the soccer ball was left in the street as we scattered. Shrapnel punctured a hole in it so now, instead of air, the soccer ball was "inflated" with newspaper.

At each end of the street, we set up empty cannon shells as our goal posts. We ran back and forth, and every now and then someone would yell "goal, goal, goal" when someone scored.

That day, in the middle of the game, Omar suggested we run down the street to see our Palestinian friends by the lighthouse. Before the words were out of his mouth, we were running at full speed toward the lighthouse. Two buildings before the lighthouse, we found our Palestinian friends and their jeep which was mounted with a 106 mm gun.

The driver was sitting in the jeep picking his teeth while looking into his rearview mirror, which he had tilted down. The other three Palestinians were sitting on the ground next to their plates with flies swarming over their leftover food.

They greeted us with smiles and the Muslim greeting, "Assalamu alaikum," which means "Peace be unto you." Omar and I walked a little closer to take a better look at the 106 mm cannon and the driver motioned to us to get into the back and check it out.

Our eyes got as big as quarters and our smiles went ear to ear. My brother Wess was sitting down by the three who were taking apart their AK-47s for cleaning.

As soon as Omar and I started to inspect the cannon, one of the three soldiers cleaning his rifle asked if we wanted to learn how to take apart an AK-47. Upon hearing that, we jumped off the jeep and knelt next to them.

They all had scruffy beards, oily olive complexions, and curly hair. As they took the weapons apart, I couldn't help but notice the grenades hooked on their vests. Each soldier had two hand grenades on the upper side of his chest, one on the upper right and the other on the upper left. The dark green hand grenades were covered in bulging squares. Each had a shiny pin with a metal arm that went down one side of it. Below the two hand grenades was a vest with six long pockets that held banana-shaped magazines.

The soldier couldn't help noticing my eyes staring at the grenades as if I wanted them on my Christmas list. He winked at me and tapped his AK-47 as if saying "Pay attention" as he began to explain the history of the gun he was holding. We were like school kids engrossed in our favorite subject.

The AK-47 was designed by Mikhail Kalashnikov, a Russian veteran. It was the most dependable weapon ever made, even to this day. It looked as if it were made for war. It has a distinctive sound when fired and is the easiest weapon to take apart and reassemble because, unlike the M-16, it had very few parts.

It was built to withstand extreme cold and could be used in muddy or sandy conditions without concern about it becoming jammed.

Cleaning it was as simple as running a knotted shoe lace dipped in motor oil through the barrel. It only takes five grains of sand to jam an M-16 while the AK-47 could be in the middle of a sandstorm without ever jamming.

Even though it was not as accurate as the M-16 for shooting targets at a distance, it made up for it by being the most dependable weapon made with a 7.62 bullet which has a very strong knock-down power.

The soldiers finished cleaning their guns and put them back together quickly. Then the demonstration started. All three, almost simultaneously, removed the top plate by pressing the button, then the spring, then the inside mechanism slid right out. We were amazed at how easy it seemed to be.

Then, as we cheered, they started showing off, seeing who could take apart his gun and put it back together the fastest.

Then, one of the guerrilla fighters asked us if we wanted to fire a few shots. Omar and I both shouted, "Me, me!"

So, he handed Omar the AK-47 and moved the lever to the semi-automatic position instead of full automatic. Omar walked a few feet from under the building and fired a shot in the air hollering, "Allahu Akbar," which means God is great in Arabic.

We cheered and, when Omar handed the gun back with a big smile on his face, we heard a weird beeping noise coming from the walkie-talkie from inside the jeep. Within a second, the soldiers' carefree smiles became worried frowns.

We knew something was wrong because they all jumped in the jeep, AK-47s in hand. The driver popped a wheel while the rest of the guerrillas rocked back and held onto the cannon mounted on the back of the jeep.

We all started to run because we could tell by their faces that something was about to happen. The jeep made a sharp left and we made a sharp right when one of the soldiers yelled, "Yella, yella" meaning come on, come on.

I slowed my fast jog to a walk to see what was happening. I could see them opening the back of the 106 mm cannon. They were trying to load it while the jeep was moving.

As soon as I saw that, my heart started to pound and so did my feet. Within seconds, I was at the heels of my brother and our friends, who reached their homes just before we reached ours.

My brother Wess was running like a deer between the parked cars and into the entrance of our building which was dark because the long, tunnel-like corridor had no lights. Coming in from bright sunlight to complete darkness made it even more difficult to focus. We needed to find the first step and from there, it was autopilot to the fifth floor. We knew those marble stairs by heart even in pitch darkness, having climbed them many times in the dark because the electricity was off so often.

After we reached the second floor, we heard a big bang from the jeep which made us go even faster. Within seconds, we were at our floor and the door was already open for us, our mother standing there in shock watching us get up the stairs so fast. She did not know, nor did we tell her, that we were aware of what the big bang was. I told her we were on the way up when we heard the bang. She said it sounded like a cannon and it was close. Wess and I looked at each other and said, "Yes, it did seem very close."

I ran to my room to get my binoculars and told my brother that we could get a better look if we went up to the roof of the building. We both smiled and headed to the door.

Wess told mom that we were going to water the plants at the neighbor's house since we had all the keys to most of the flats. We ran out the door and headed up. As we passed the owner's floor, the eighth floor with all those climbing plants covering the walls, I started to unzip my pants.

Wess looked at me as if I were crazy and, when I said to him that the owner of this building was Syrian, he also unzipped his pants and we pissed in every single plant that he had. After all, I reasoned, it was the Syrian bombardment that killed our Nana and destroyed her home.

After our pit stop, we continued toward the apartment on the eighth floor where the French lady lived with her cat. Next to her door was a gray steel ladder and behind the ladder was the elevator room.

As Wess and I climbed up the ladder, we heard another bang. I quickly reached the steel door and pushed it several times to get it open. It was frozen in place as if no one had opened it in a while.

We finally made it onto the roof. As our eyes were adjusting to the light, we couldn't help but notice pieces of shrapnel scattered all over the roof. Most of the pieces were rusty, but some were recent because they still had that shiny, silvery look. I started to look with my binoculars towards the sea while Wess started to pick up shrapnel, putting them in his pockets.

"Oh, my God, Wess, look!" I yelled as I handed him the glasses.

Only about a mile out sat two huge battleships. I took the glasses back, focusing to get a clearer look when we heard five or six pops. They weren't that loud, but within seconds, shells were whistling over us and landing a block from us.

And, yes, those were loud, very loud. We both got back on the ladder like firemen and almost broke our necks because we landed on top of each other. But, there was no time for pain.

The building shook and we heard screams coming from flats as we passed by. The elevator doors rattled; then we heard mom yelling our names in the stairwell. We were coming from the opposite end. She was mad and scared and said, "What the hell were you doing upstairs?"

Wess and I told her that the battleships were firing on us. She had our little brother Dani in one hand and our emergency bag in the other.

Inside the bag were all our passports, my dad's Smith and Wesson 38 caliber handgun, my mom's jewelry, and two big bars of gold, which I didn't know about until later. Soma was standing behind my mother crying.

We stayed by the elevator door, the safest place to be. We heard eight more pops, which came from the Israeli gunboat, and then the explosions started. We didn't hear the whistling noise this time because they were landing in our street and on the rooftops of the buildings around us. Glass started to break and you could hear shrapnel bouncing off our walls. Wess said to me that they were trying to hit the jeep that was firing on them earlier.

# Chapter 13
## A Secret Stash

After living in a war zone, you learn that when you hear the whistling noise from the shells, it means that they passed over you and when you don't, you better hit the ground because they are very close if not on top of you.

More pops came from the gunboats and more shells landed on top of the buildings around us and then we heard this horrible scream coming from our street.

I looked at my mom and started to tell her what a piece of shit my dad was. I was mad and scared, but this time, the anger had built up more than ever. The look on my mother's face was shock. Even so, she was shaking her head as if she agreed with me; so, I let it all out.

I called him every name in the book. How could that asshole get to travel all over the world while we were sitting here with bombs raining on us, with no water or electricity, everyone gone, and we are left to die. Then I took a deep breath and said that that son of a bitch should at least be with us to see what we are going through every day.

Everyone was quiet as I walked back into the house and went to my room. My mom kept saying, "Come back here," but I didn't care. I went to my room and straight to the balcony to see what the damage was in our street.

To my surprise, I saw TV antennas all in the street, some still dangling from the roof tops. Apparently some of the shells landed on the roof of the building adjacent to ours, cutting down all the TV antennas except for one. Some smoke was coming from down the street, but it didn't look terrible. Wess started to count all the windows that were broken and we could see there were a lot of them.

It was quiet that evening and we found out that the scream we heard was from a live-in maid, just like Soma, who died from shrapnel wounds. Most of the live-in maids in Lebanon were from Sri Lanka, India, or the Philippines. And why they were sent to Lebanon to work, I could never understand. They would have a better chance on death row than in Beirut.

That night we lit our candles and our bright kerosene lamps and did what we did every night. We lit up our Katol mosquito repellent and started playing cards. Our favorite game was War.

While we were playing, I told Wess I wish there was a store open because I was craving chewing gum. During the Israeli invasion, you were lucky if you could get bread, much less chewing gum.

He jumped up and said, "I have gum," and I replied, "You do?" as if it was a miracle. Then, the next few words out of his mouth were, "I'll sell you some."

I started to turn red and I didn't want to show him how angry I was because I couldn't believe that he was going to sell me a piece of gum. I said, "Ok, go get it."

He said I had to stay where I was because he didn't want anyone knowing where his stash was.

I could see his flashlight shining in our bedroom and, after a few minutes, he returned with the gum. He reached out his empty hand first as if saying "Show me the money" and that's when I started to punch him!

I finally got to grab the gum out of his other hand. While playing cards went flying everywhere, my mom came running to separate us, and after telling her what happened, she sent us to bed That's when I gave him his nickname, "Jew Boy."

The next day, I asked my mother if Wess was really related to us and how could anyone be that tight? She laughed and said that God made everyone different.

He and I didn't talk for days after that.

# Chapter 14
## And Dani said, "Bad dogs, bad dogs."

While the city was under siege, Israeli jets flew by one afternoon and, to our surprise, it was raining pink papers all over the city, especially onto Al-Hamra Street, a few blocks away from us.

Al-Hamra Street was where all the nice stores and movie theaters as well as bars and prostitutes were. During the invasion, most of the stores were either closed or barricaded by sandbags, but the bars and prostitutes stayed in business.

We ran to Al-Hamra after we saw a few kids running and yelling, waving the pink flyers in their hands. We finally got one and some kids wanted ours, too, so the yelling started. Right before things got out of control, Max, our neighborhood dog, darted right past us and started barking at the other kids. They started to run in all directions, thanks to our canine guardian angel. The funny thing was that we didn't even see him follow us.

All of a sudden, gunfire erupted everywhere. It was Palestinian guerillas shooting in the air to stop people from picking up the leaflets. We started to walk home and I slipped the leaflet into my pocket just as others on the street did regardless of the warning by the guerillas.

As we passed by one of the soldiers who was firing in the air, I walked up to him and asked him if he could give me a bullet as a souvenir. He smiled, reached into his army green pockets which were almost overflowing with AK-47 bullets and, to my surprise, gave me a handful of them. Wess and two of our friends did the same and they got the same. We ran home smiling as if someone had given us diamonds.

As we reached our street, Max went to his favorite spot to lie down and we started to hear more anti-aircraft fire erupt into the air. And, since we got to hear it every day, we didn't run or panic.

When we got home, we showed my mom the leaflet that said, "If you leave the city now, you will not get hurt. However, if you stay, we are not responsible" or something to that effect.

After mom looked at it, she smiled and gave it back to me. I proceeded to the balcony where Wess and I lit the leaflet on fire and let it fall from the fifth floor. Omar saw what we were doing and pointed to the trash pile, which was more than ready to burn. I told mom that we were going to burn the trash and to start heating our water on the gas stove so we could shower.

That made her happy and with a smile on her face she said, "Hurry up." She was always on us about showering no matter what was going on, especially with Wess, now "Jew Boy," because he hated showers.

We met Omar by the huge trash pile and he had a bottle of gasoline in his hand and a grin on his face which meant that he siphoned it from someone's car. I climbed into the middle of the trash pile and looked up towards our balcony to make sure my mom wasn't watching me waist deep in trash with a bottle of gasoline in one hand and a book of matches in the other, trying to balance myself.

There were flies and roaches everywhere and I finally felt that I was standing on something sturdy. I started to dump the gasoline all around me and the roaches started to run because they could either smell the gasoline or they could taste it. I threw the empty bottle back to Omar and went to strike a match to it when I dropped the book of matches.

I looked down, and as I got closer to where the book of matches landed, I noticed that I was standing on some metal object with serial numbers on it in English. I removed a trash bag which started to rip and discovered that I was standing on an unexploded shell. It looked like a bullet that was taller than I was and three feet wide.

My eyes got big and raising both of my arms in the air, I yelled, "Stop, stop, stop. It's a bomb. Don't light anything!" Everyone got closer to where I was standing, which was right on it.

I jumped off like a crazy man trying to say something and no one understood the words coming out of my mouth. My mouth was dry and my heart was pounding. Everyone got a closer look and started a chain of "Oh, God. We could have blown up our neighborhood!"

From all the commotion, people started to look out of their balconies to see what all the yelling was about. Within a few minutes, there were twenty people or more pointing at the bullet-shaped bomb. Apparently, it came from the Israeli gunboats when they bombed us earlier in the day and the pile of trash softened the blow preventing it from detonating. An older man told us we'd better leave just in case it blew up. Everyone went home.

That night, we told our mom about it and she shook her head and walked to the balcony to see what we were talking about. And there it was. From the fifth floor, you could see it as clear as day, lying on its side and gray in color. I told Wess I wished it was a lot smaller so we could add it to our collection of bullets and shrapnel. Mom heard me and said, "You're crazy! The water is ready. Go take your showers."

That night, we heard on the radio that there was a ceasefire and that the United Nations was going to bring in flour and food to the city. Soon after we heard that, we knew that we had to get up at the crack of dawn to stand in line for bread at the bakery, which was next to the mosque and the church behind our house.

My brother and I were excited to at least get out of the house and take care of the family. We had a plan. When we were in the bread line, we would not stand together because they were only giving each family ten flat, thin loaves of bread; that way, we could get twenty.

Later that night, Wess and I talked about how much gunpowder that bomb would have in it compared to the bullets that we already had. During the invasion we had learned to open up the bullets, take out the gunpowder, trace our names on the concrete with the gunpowder, and then put a match to it. It was the coolest thing to do, we thought. By using two pairs of pliers to slowly twist the casing from the bullet, we could take the gunpowder out. It only took a second to write anything you wanted on concrete with the gunpowder and once lit, it stayed there for years.

That night was one of the quietest until we heard a bunch of wild dogs barking in our street. It was so annoying that I went onto our balcony to throw something at them, like a small flower pot. I knew if my mom found out that I used one of her flower pots, I would never hear the end of it. So, I looked around for something else to throw when I saw something shiny in the corner of our balcony next to my chopper bike. It was one of my little brother Dani's Matchbox cars. I hurled it at the dogs from the fifth floor. It landed right in the middle of them and went into pieces. They all froze for just a second, then went back to barking at each other and I could see what the problem was.

Max wasn't around because if he were, none of this would have been happening. One dog was in charge, I could tell, because if he approached the other dogs, they would cower and put their tails between their legs. And now I could see why the barking and the fighting was taking place: a male dog was trying to hump a dog while another dog was trying to stop it. So, the angry one would bite the dog in the back while he was trying to hump his girl. He would stop for a few seconds, wait until the angry dog looked in the other direction, and the same thing would happen again. It was as if I were watching the Discovery Channel, live from our balcony.

I guess I wasn't the only one watching this. The building across from us now housed mostly Palestinian refugees. Two of them waved at me, so I waved at them and they pointed at the dogs. I shook my head. Then, one of them held up his finger as if saying, "Wait a minute."

He went back inside. I figured that he was going to get something to throw at them, so I looked back down at the dogs. They seemed to have surrounded a cat that was yowling in pain. Out of the center of the pack came a big black dog, so black you could barely see him except for his white teeth. The poor cat was in his mouth.

Then came the distinctive sound of an AK-47 being cocked which completely got my attention. I looked up and there was the man who had waved at me earlier. He smiled at me and all I could do was take a step back and give him the thumbs up. As he pointed his AK-47 down towards the dogs, a burst of rounds blasted through the air, the empty shell casings hitting the ground as a big flash came out of the barrel like a mad dragon, all in the blink of an eye.

Then the howling started, a terrible howl. I didn't want to look, but I could hear the panic of all the other dogs by the screeching of their paws as they ran off. I could hear the ones that were shot, the ones that were making that awful high-pitched howling.

And then it was quiet except for one dog whose howls became fainter and fainter the farther away he went.

I got to my bed and Wess and Dani asked me, "How many did they shoot?" I told them three or more, but I really didn't look.

I looked at the watch lying by my bed by pushing the light button. It was twelve midnight. I told Wess we had four hours before we had to go to the bakery.

Dani asked if they were good dogs or bad dogs and I said they were bad. He lay back in his bed half asleep and said in a low voice, "They were bad dogs."

Wess and I started to giggle because Dani was still dreaming, and kept saying "bad dogs, bad dogs."

# Chapter 15
## Bread Lines, a "Black Bird," and Baskets of News

A few hours later, at four a.m., my watch started beeping. Then we heard the loud speakers from the mosque calling for Morning Prayer and knew it was time to go. So, Wess and I got up, got the money off the kitchen counter where mom had left it, and went out the door as quietly as two thieves in the night.

Before we headed down the stairs, I reminded Wess about our pit stop, so we went up three stories and pissed in all the flower pots of the building owner, and, since we hadn't peed all night, it was enough for all of them. Not only did we piss in them because he was Syrian, but because during the winter months, he would cut the heat off and try to ask for more money for heating oil and all the tenants were upset. In a way, peeing in his flower pots was for everyone.

After finishing our pissing contest, we headed down the stairs. It was still a little dark when we came out of our building and we felt as if we were on a mission. We took the shortcut behind our house which took us right next to the mosque.

The smell of baking bread in the air made us both drool. We passed the entrance of the mosque and saw five people already in line. I reminded Wess to act as if we didn't know each other so we could get more bread as they only gave one allotment to each family.

I let an older lady get in front of me while Wess was in another line not too far from me. We stood there for a few minutes and watched the line behind us getting longer and longer by the minute.

Wess got his ten loaves of pita bread and then walked down the street where I could see him waiting for me. After the older lady got her bread, I was next. I got my ten loaves and headed toward Wess. I looked behind me and the line was getting even longer, trailing all the way to the church across the street from the mosque. Wess said that we were lucky that we got there early or we would have been there for hours.

By the time we headed home, the sun was shining through the buildings and it was nice and quiet, the speakers from the mosque and the crowing roosters having finished their early morning calls.

We got home and mom had our chocolate milk ready for us in the kitchen. Soma had her bed folded in half and was getting ready to help my mother with cleaning the house. I told my mom that we should be able to play outside a lot longer today since there was a ceasefire between the Palestinians and the Israelis.

Wess, Dani, and I went to the balcony to clean our bikes. The salt air from the Mediterranean would eat right through the metal if we didn't keep them clean. We were on our knees rubbing the chrome polisher between all the tire spokes when we heard the pops from the gun boats.

Big-eyed and on our feet in a flash, we grabbed out our little brother's arms from each side and ran inside. Mom and Soma were heading towards the door so we could get near the elevator where it was the safest when the shells landed. The building shook as the shells exploded, glass shattered in our kitchen, and Wess yelled, "Ceasefire? What kind of ceasefire is this?"

Three more pops were heard and the building shook again. They were very close because you could hear the shrapnel bouncing off the walls outside. We smelled smoke; then there was an eerie quiet followed by a siren from the Red Cross.

I walked back to the kitchen to take a peek because I knew we had a broken window. I could see the smoke coming from the back balcony. My mom and Wess were right behind me waiting for some more pops, but it never happened. My mom and Soma started to sweep the glass while Wess and I kept Dani out of the kitchen so he wouldn't step in it or cut himself.

Wess went back to the balcony to pick up the bikes because they had fallen from the concussion of the shells. Mom said the smoke was coming from between the buildings and the mosque. Wess and I looked at each other because that is where we were just a few hours ago to get bread.

More sirens came and they all seemed to be headed in the same direction, one street over from us where we picked up our bread.

As soon as Soma and my mom got all the glass up, Wess and I took our positions on the back balcony with our binoculars to get a better look. We couldn't see anything but smoke because the mosque was in the way. But we heard some noises coming from right behind our building.

We stood up on some crates so we could see over the chest-high balcony wall. What we saw were some Palestinian gunmen holding a white sheet with something black in it, something like a black bird.

We called my mom and she looked and so did Soma, but we still couldn't tell what it was. Later we found out that what looked like a black bird hanging out of the sheet was the head of the old lady who had been standing in the bread line with us that morning. She had been killed by fire from the Israeli gunboats, her head severed from her body.

It was such a horrible image that we didn't talk about it and it was never brought up again.

* * *

The next morning, we let the basket down to get the newspaper. It was a neighborhood invention. Everyone put money in a small basket and dangled it from the balcony to the sidewalk each morning for the paper man. Since there was no electricity, he was not going to the fifth floor or any other floor for that matter. He would come at 6:00 a.m., the quietest part of the day except for the rumbling of his French-made Vespa motorcycle with leather pouches holding tightly-wrapped newspapers. He would cruise by slowly and all the baskets would come dangling down.

The cool thing about getting the paper for me was not the reading part, but the photos of the devastation all around us. The whole paper was packed with action shots of bombs exploding and buildings collapsing from the new vacuum bombs dropped by Israeli jets. Fifteen stories could be brought down to the ground without messing up the top floor. That's when the U.S. was trying to test them and we were the test grounds. A few that didn't explode had engravings of where they were made and they all said U.S.A. along with the name of the state in which they were made.

Now the daily newspaper headlines for those two weeks of bombardment from the Israeli gunboats were: Black Monday, Black Tuesday, Black Wednesday, and so on for each day during the siege. Photos of tanks that were hit with rocket-propelled grenades as well as famous restaurants like the Nasser on the cliffs of the Mediterranean hit by the gunboats filled up its pages.

The owner of the Nasser Restaurant was a good friend of my father. My dad used to take us there a lot and the owner, Mr. Nasser, would come to our house on many occasions and have lunch with us. I could never forget the toys he brought with him: bicycles, cars, stuffed animals.

As the days dragged by and the gunfire became less constant, my mother decided to sign me up for some more English classes at the ACS with a tutor a couple hours a week. At first I thought she was crazy, but when I thought about it, I realized that I could get the hell out of the house. So I smiled and said "Yes, I would be glad to go." It was only a ten minute walk from our building and, at nine in the morning, it was still quiet except for a few bursts of anti-aircraft fire here and there.

On my walk to school to meet my new tutor, I saw Palestinian fighters cleaning their guns as I took my usual short cut beside the Saudi Embassy. The stairs were very long but wide and, after smiling at the soldiers and them nodding back, I began to smell a bad odor.

As I walked down the stairs, the odor got stronger. Then, there it was: a dog lying there with flies all over the holes in its body. I covered my mouth when one of the soldiers said, "Don't be scared. He was going to eat one of us last night."

I picked up the pace and covered my mouth with my hand. The cologne that I was wearing helped lessen the horrible odor in the air. I reached the school and my teacher was there at the gate. He was a tall man with brown hair and a little big in the middle. We got to know each other better after a few weeks and started to talk about the war and the Israeli invasion. He asked me what I did to keep myself occupied since we didn't have any electricity. I told him I liked to collect bullets and shrapnel. He grinned as if he were thinking "boys will be boys."

"When you come back, bring them with you so I can see what kind of collection you have" he said.

I nodded my head and said, "No problem," as I headed out the door.

# Chapter 16
## PLO Agrees to Leave Beirut and Father Returns

Two days later, there was an announcement made on the radio that the ceasefire would lead to the evacuation of all PLO fighters and their leader, Yasser Arafat. Most of the Palestinians wanted to stay and fight to the end. Many of them said this is where they could beat the enemy, in street-to-street fighting, in which the Israelis had little experience. Also, the Israeli air force would be of no use if both sides were fighting each other in the streets. And, they said, tanks could be easily taken out in the narrow streets of Beirut as the Israelis would find out. It seems our city was a better place to wage their battles than their own. Who cared that our citizens were suffering?

With the Palestinians being pushed out, food and aid was sent into Beirut by the U.N. Within a few days, we got a phone call from my father saying that he was coming by way of Syria in a taxi since there was a ceasefire. First, I couldn't believe that the phone rang because the phone hadn't worked in months even before we accidentally melted the phone box while burning the trash piles. Apparently, our building wasn't affected.

We got word that the Israeli army was opening up some roads to the city to let some people in, like women and children. As soon as my mother heard that, we jumped into the Volkswagen bug and drove to see if we could cross from West Beirut to East Beirut. There was a major crossing point by the racetrack.

As we drove through the city, my brother and I were awed by the destruction and devastation. In some streets there was nothing left but rubble and skeletons of what used to be cars. Some streets we didn't recognize. Almost every street had a big pile of dirt at the end of it to obscure the view and protect the soldiers from being seen.

We finally reached the major checkpoint to cross into East Beirut when we saw a huge Israeli tank with soldiers all around it. We had never seen Israeli soldiers or an Israeli tank before. As we got closer to the checkpoint, my brother and I were mesmerized by the size of that tank with the tallest antenna mounted on the back of it. It was parked on an angle and the gun turret was pointed in our direction.

When we got to the Israeli soldier, we saw how clean he was, how his facial features were similar to ours, and that he even had a smile on his face. We had thought an Israeli soldier would be a dirty, evil-looking person with a scruffy beard. He looked inside our car, winked at us, and waved us through.

As soon as we passed the checkpoint, the racetrack was on our right, or what used to be a racetrack. Some parts of the wall that went around the place were knocked down and we could see bits and pieces of track. Suddenly, our car swerved to the left barely missing a huge crater in the ground which was just as big as our car.

After arriving at my cousin's, only a block from the racetrack, my heart started to pound from the excitement of being out of our neighborhood and into the outside world. Plus, my cousin Walid was the master of building tanks and castles and forts out of wood. Most of all, they lived on the top floor of their building which overlooked the whole area, including the racetrack. In the past, we could even ride bikes on his balcony it was so long.

We were only there for about two hours when the radio announced that the ceasefire has started falling apart. My brother thought and hoped this would be a good excuse to get stuck at my cousin's house. But, before we could say anything, we were back in the car and on the way home.

My mother was popping wheels and driving like a racecar driver while trying to avoid bomb craters that could swallow the car with us in it. We got through the checkpoint, but this time, the soldiers that had been standing around the tank were now all in it with their helmets on, tank engine running, and none of the smiles that we saw before. Within ten minutes, we were on our street driving around the huge mounds of dirt that blocked the street from direct view of the Israeli destroyers there in the Mediterranean.

Running up five flights of stairs, my brother and I got there first, panting and out of breath. We ran to our room to get the binoculars, man our positions on the balcony, and see who could spot the destroyer first.

It took my mother a few minutes longer to get to the fifth floor carrying Dani. Just as I spotted the destroyer, we heard a loud swooshing noise that startled us. We saw the reflection of flames on the adjacent glass windows and realized it was a rocket launcher firing some forty rockets from the soccer fields.

The Syrians were firing rockets right over our building that disappeared into the sky. The rockets seemed to pass slowly over our building and then they would accelerate at a much faster speed once they cleared us. We weren't as scared now that we knew these rockets were outgoing and not incoming. Instead, we were excited. Every time the rocket launcher would fire, we would yell as it took off from one side of the balcony, then run to the back balcony to see it disappear into the sky. They looked like big suppositories in the sky with one big roar followed by another. Some would be released slowly with a few seconds between them. The ones we looked forward to were the ones that were released so fast that you couldn't even count them.

Our balconies turned into communication lines to everything around us. We were advised not to pick up any toys or even gold pens that could explode in your hands causing severe injuries and death. It happened a lot. Kids would find a new soccer ball left on the field, start to kick it around, and a few minutes later, a loud explosion and three kids were dead.

The next day brought another ceasefire. It was very quiet except for the occasional wild dogs running in the street either chasing a cat or being chased by Max.

A yellow cab pulled up and I could hear my dad's voice. I rubbed my eyes because I couldn't believe my father had arrived. From the fifth floor, we started to run down to meet him knowing that he had a long way up with two big suitcases plus a smaller one for his navigation charts and emergency equipment. Even more important was the tall jar of honey which he always had with him, more important to him than the Jumbo 747 he flew. It was a mainstay of his diet and he put it in and on everything!

We helped him with the suitcases until we reached the fifth floor, exhausted and out of breath, but we knew that somewhere inside one of those suitcases were gifts for us.

Before my father reached our floor, my mother told us not to tell him how bad it really was in the invasion. Wess and I looked at each other and smiled. We wanted him to see what it was like to run for cover and piss in your pants at the same time. We had been shelled and bombed, lived without electricity and water for months, and all this time, he was outside the country. Watching it on TV was not the same as living in the war zone where an F-18 was your alarm clock dropping bombs all over the city and what looked like a flock of birds was anti-aircraft fire. So, now it was his time to hear and see the things that we had experienced for the past few months.

That night it was quiet so we did our nighttime rituals: taking our showers standing on the tile floors with a small bucket in one hand and soap in the other, lighting the candles in all the rooms, and setting up a little table on the balcony so we could play cards and not miss anything going on in the street below. Being on the fifth floor afforded us a bird's-eye view of all the buildings and streets around us clear up to the Saudi Arabian embassy.

Most of the people in the buildings around us were refugees. There was always a commotion going on, something to hear or see: someone fighting with his wife, coughing, candles being lit, etc. Once we saw someone trying to pump up a kerosene lamp when it went up in a bright fireball. Luckily, he was able to toss it from the tenth floor all the way down to the middle of the street. Anything that we saw or heard was a diversion for us since we were so bored.

We showed our dad our bullets and shrapnel collection. He was very impressed and tried to tell us that it was dangerous to have live ammunition in the house. We stuffed them back in the hiding place that we had before he changed his mind and made us throw them away. He had no idea that our streets were filled with them, but we didn't want to ruin his surprise.

While staring out of the balcony, I heard a little whistle and, even though it was dark, I could tell that it was coming from Omar's house. I made a little whistle back and shined my flashlight until I found him on his balcony right over the coffee shop, a big hangout where older people liked to play backgammon and smoke their Lebanese hookahs. Omar was trying to tell me something with his hands, but I couldn't make it out until he made the rocket launcher noise and pointed to the direction of the soccer field. My ears perked up and I waited.

In recent weeks, we had seen how they loaded the rocket launcher before it was fired. Two men, sometimes three men depending on the size of the rockets, would pick up the front of the rocket first and then the back end. Very carefully the front man would line up the front of the rocket into one of the many holes in the launcher. Once it was loaded, he would quickly go to the back of the rocket to help push the whole thing in and connect some wiring to arm it. It looked like a long process depending on how many soldiers there were.

That night, my brother Wess and I waited for hours until that loud roar finally started and you could see the big flashes in the sky with a screeching noise that faded as it passed across the sky towards the Israeli positions. Within seconds, we heard a thump, and my dad came stumbling into our room in the dark yelling, "Get up! We need to go to the bomb shelter now!

As the loud screeching noise came to an end, we started to giggle and said to him, "Welcome to Beirut!"

My mom followed him into our room saying to him, "Toufic, go back to sleep. Those were 'outgoing'."

He asked her, "What do you mean 'outgoing'?" as he turned and ran smack into the edge of the door on his way out.

That night was the best sleep we had had since the invasion. Morning came and my mother and father started breakfast. We decided to have it on the balcony where between some buildings you could see the deep blue Mediterranean.

Only two blocks away and not far from shore were the gray Israeli gunboats. It was so unusual not to hear any gunfire or the regular anti-aircraft pops, like a million giant bags of popcorn exploding in the sky. Everyone else was on their balconies waving good morning to us.

Hearing the Vespa motorcycle, everyone ran to the balconies' edges and dropped down their baskets. It was time to get the paper. The noisy Vespa grew louder which meant it was closer to our street, its rumbling echoing off every building. Like hamsters sniffing the air, people leaned their bodies over the edges of the railings as if trying to see around a corner, an improbability, but we all did it anyway. Finally, the paper guy was on our street and dozens of baskets came dangling down as if each one was saying, "Me first!"

My brother lowered our basket with the money and waited for the paper guy to tug on the line like a fish that had swallowed a hook. To us, the paper was our connection to the outside world and how that world was viewing the invasion of Lebanon.

Then came the best part: the pictures, pictures of buildings and famous landmarks that were heavily damaged or completely destroyed by airstrikes. The coliseum, a huge arena with ancient statues of Roman athletes as well as ancient columns, was blown apart after an Israeli jet dropped a bunker buster that ignited the ammunition storage put there by the Palestinians, the explosions causing heavy casualties to both civilian populations and structures for miles.

Since rockets were flying in all directions, indiscriminately hitting buildings and cars for an entire week, the newspaper pictures covered large areas. We studied every detail in the pictures, guessing as to whether the target was hit from air, land, or water. Depending on the size of the crater and even the angle of shrapnel, we could tell from which direction it came.

While Wess was on the floor with the paper spread out, I walked to the balcony where my dad was drinking his coffee and staring into the sea. We heard what sounded like pops in the distance and before I could sip my cup of milk, everything started to go in slow motion: glass shattering, Wess army-crawling across the floor toward the door, my mother running out of the kitchen with Dani in one arm and pointing to the door with the other.

Explosion after explosion shook the building. I was at the door with my dad unlocking all the deadbolts. It was like trying to escape from a lion when he was in the room with you.

We poured into the area by the elevator when more pops were heard followed by more loud, deafening explosions, the bouncing of shrapnel, screams, and the shattering of glass ringing in my ears.

# Chapter 17
## Israeli Jet Fighter Shot Down

They say a picture is worth a thousand words. All I had to do was look at my dad's face, pale white, his eyes filled with terror. He was trying to keep us all together while debating if we should take a chance and run to the bomb shelter five stories down or wait to see if we heard any more pops.

Suddenly, someone yelled, "It's from the Israeli gunboats." We had no whistling shells to give us warning as they were firing directly at us, not over us. It took a few hours for our nerves to calm down. Then, without anyone speaking, everyone started to pick up debris and straighten up the mess that was created in the chaos. People came out to see where the shells hit. All you had to do was follow the smoke. I started to notice that every day at three p.m., the Israeli gunboats would appear on the horizon, move in closer, and then start shelling.

Wess and I talked my father into going to our grandmother's so he could check on the huge garden that he and my uncle had turned into a fruit and vegetable paradise. It was surrounded by razor wire and had broken glass imbedded into the top of the stone walls. It didn't take much to convince him, especially when we said that it was even safer than our house because the walls were three feet thick and all the windows were covered in sandbags. It wouldn't take but a drop of gas, we continued to plead, since it was only three blocks away.

Finally, we were in the car going around the barriers and huge potholes and within two minutes, we were at Teta's. I was so happy to be there with my cousins in our grandmother's bunker protected by three-foot thick walls and sandbagged windows. We compared stories and traded the bullets we were collecting the way American kids trade baseball cards.

While we were catching up on things, my dad and Uncle Hussein were gathering vegetables from the garden and watering it. Their watering system began with two concrete pools filled with water from the well that my grandfather had dug many years ago. Once my father turned the valve, the water rushed out of the pools into the channels which were trenched by hand and led to every tree and plant. It was like studying a maze as we watched the water follow its path.

Within an hour of being at Teta's, the Israeli gunboats opened fire. Their shells started to whistle over us followed by explosions. Everyone ran to the bunker.

My brother Wess and our cousins got there first. Once she felt the concussion from the exploding shells, Teta, who had been sitting in the front room, quickly headed to the bunker followed by my father and Uncle Hussein, who were the last ones to get in because they were at the other side of the garden.

As soon as they got in, a shell exploded nearby and shrapnel was heard bouncing off the sandbags. There was a break for a few seconds, and that's when another uncle ran in with a briefcase in his arms and tears in his eyes.

We called him Uncle Chiclets because he owned a small grocery store and every time we walked by from school, he would offer us Chiclets. He was always smiling, but not today. He was sitting in a chair rocking his body back and forth and holding his briefcase close to his chest as if fearing that someone was going to take it away from him.

More shells landed behind our building. Then, it got quiet, and as soon as we started to wonder if it was finally over, machine gun fire erupted. We could hear bullets bouncing off cars and hitting glass, car tires popping, and metal rattling all up and down the street. We thought that the gunboats had gotten so close to the shoreline that they were using the boat's deck guns.

After it was over, one of my older cousins stepped out with his AK-47 in hand to check out the damage. We peered out the door since all the windows were blocked by sandbags. My dad pointed at two silver-colored pieces of shrapnel lying right outside the front door. You could see where they had punctured the bags from the trail of sand spilling out.

My dad yelled at my little brother Dani as he went to grab the shrapnel. Wess and I knew to wait for them to cool down, a lesson Dani would learn for the first time that day. When a shell explodes, pieces of hot metal called shrapnel shoot out in all directions. When they are hot, they look just like newly-polished silver, but, as they cool, they turn gray, and, after two days, they start to rust.

Within minutes, we could hear my cousins cussing loudly. We waited for my dad to step outside. We followed a few feet behind him because we didn't want him to yell at us, but we wanted to see what was happening. But, we didn't need to worry because he was so distracted by what he saw and the continuous cussing of my cousins that he never paid us any attention.

There were bullets in every car all the way up and down the street. We could see the Mediterranean to our left, and I squinted my eyes and saw the gunboats were no longer there. We all took a deep breath since things had quieted down except for now my father and cousins and more people joined in with the cussing.

We noticed that all the bullet holes were on one side of all the cars. The fronts of the cars were facing the sea, and there were no holes in the front. My older cousin walked away from the cars where he had found hundreds of empty shell casings all over the other side of the street.

Now, like a "Columbo" episode, the case had been solved. Apparently, while all the shelling has been going on, some Palestinian fighters took advantage of the situation, stood across the street and, without discrimination, sprayed all the cars with bullets and left. It was their farewell gift to us, something else to remember them by.

My brother and I started to check out our VW bug. It only had two bullet holes in the door, so we started to check out my cousin's car which had so many more. While he waved his AK-47 in the air, we felt the holes with our fingers the way a blind man does with Braille, giggling at all the cuss words they were yelling out, an encyclopedia to us because some we had never heard and some were used on a daily basis by everyone in the family, especially my uncles.

I started to pick up some shell casings from the spot where they had been fired, when my uncle's wife came out to the balcony and yelled, "They shot one down, they shot one down!"

Everyone stopped what they were doing and ran towards the building to see what was shot down. Then, a cousin from an adjacent building said an F-18 was just shot down by anti-aircraft fire.

I was so excited that I dropped all the empty shell casings out of my hands and ran behind my cousin. He was the only one who had a five inch black and white TV which was hooked up to a car battery in the bunker at my grandmother's house. He put the safety on the AK-47, slid it under the bed, and started to connect the TV wires to the car battery.

There were ten of us trying to squeeze our heads in to look at a five-inch screen. The sound came on first with a newscaster speaking. Then, it took a few minutes for the little screen to warm up and the picture slowly started to get brighter. The announcer kept saying that an Israeli fighter jet was shot down by anti-aircraft fire and then they showed the pilot in the middle of the street surrounded by older men and women who were all taking turns kicking him.

A woman reached in, yelled in his face, and proceeded to slap him across the face several times until another man pushed her away and had his turn at punching and kicking the pilot. The camera filming was very shaky, the photographer being jostled by the angry mob trying to reach the pilot. As far as they were concerned, the pilot had been bombing their city and now it was payback time and they didn't want anyone in their way, including the cameraman.

After a few seconds, the cameraman was able to get a better shot of the pilot. He still had his parachute hooked up to his straps and his head was moving from side to side with each punch. He looked unconscious.

Shortly after that, the crowd parted and we could see what looked like a black Ford Bronco backing up at full speed, almost running over the pilot. Two Palestinian fighters jumped out, grabbed the pilot, and threw him in the back of the truck as if he were a big bag of flour. Shoving his parachute in with him, they lifted the gate with one swoop and got into the truck as the people chanted "God Is Great! Allahu Akbar" over and over as the truck sped away.

I pulled my head out from the row of heads in front of the little TV and ran outside yelling the same thing as the crowd, that God was the greatest. After all the fear the fighter jets had caused us during all those months of bombing, finally, one had been shot down.

Everyone in Beirut was celebrating by firing their guns in the air. Every time a newscaster announced the news about the downed Israeli jet, people ran to their balconies with their AK-47s, M-16s, pistols, or heavy machine guns and fired into the air. It was as if we had won the war by only shooting down one plane.

We got home with the two bullet holes in our VW, but it was okay because the jet had been shot down. We ran up the stairs to the fifth floor as fast as we could, my brother and I gasping for enough breath to tell our mother what happened, but she didn't seem to be as excited as we were.

From the balcony, we saw why it was taking my father so long to get upstairs. He had both of the car doors open and was checking where the bullets entered the car and where they exited.

In the distance, we started to hear anti-aircraft fire and as the sound got closer, my brother and I ran to our positions on the back balcony of our house. With binoculars in one hand and spray bottles in the other, we watched as Israeli jets passed over our building, the four anti-aircraft guns from the Syrian positions at the soccer field opening fire.

Within seconds, people started to shoot at the jets from their balconies, something we'd never seen before. We had to duck behind our solid concrete balcony wall because every balcony and window had a gun, pistol, and even a shotgun poised in the direction of the jet fighter.

The building across the street from us, the one full of refugees, had everyone living there shooting at the jet. There was even a small child pointing a B-B gun that was taller than he was. I started to laugh and so did my brother when after the jets were long gone, still one little gun fired into the air. The funny part was that it sounded like a 25 caliber, the smallest girlie gun you could imagine.

We could hear other people laughing on their balconies and pointing at where they thought the gunfire was coming from. Now we knew that the whole city was happy to have finally downed just one Israeli jet fighter. Even though we were still living in the worst conditions, we all felt somewhat vindicated. From bombing our electric and water stations to the killing of innocent civilians, like the elderly woman in the bread line, to the displacement of families inside and outside of Lebanon, they were the cause of our pain and suffering.

# Chapter 18
## The Feather Man

One morning, while dangling our baskets from the balconies to get the newspaper, we noticed something new in our neighborhood: a tall man with a hat decorated with bright, colorful feathers, carrying a big stick tipped with more colorful feathers and covered in colored tape. He was standing by the big pile of trash in our street sifting in and around it.

He then constructed a small cardboard box that he crawled into and went to sleep. We figured that he was a homeless man, like many others we had seen, but no one we'd seen was as colorful as this guy.

One morning, the mayor of our street, who owned the coffee shop right across from our building, approached the Feather Man and began talking to him. We couldn't hear what they were saying, but they shook hands and the Feather Man nodded as if saying, "Thank you."

Within a few days, the Feather Man was sweeping our street and washing the mayor's car, using only one bucket since the water was rationed. After all, we were at war.

One quiet morning with no gun or anti-aircraft fire, I gave a whistle and my friend Omar poked his head out of their first floor balcony across the street. He said, "Come down and play."

I asked my mother, but she said "no" remembering what happened the last time she said "yes" when it was quiet. I went back to the balcony to let Omar know she wouldn't let me. He put both hands up in the air as if saying, "Why?"

I didn't want my mother to hear or see my reply, so I pointed to my temple twirling my finger around as if to say she's "cuckoo" or "crazy."

He smiled and looked down towards where the Feather Man was sleeping in his box. A group of kids that we had never seen before were circling him. One kid grabbed his feather stick. When he got out of his cardboard box and found that the stick was gone, he chased them down the street and grabbed the stick from one of the kids. They surrounded him and one of them threw a rock at him. After that, he started karate chopping them and all five kids started screaming. He punched one kid in the stomach while side-kicking another. Finally, crying and in severe pain from the force of his blows, they all took off running and never came back.

That showed us a side of him we had not seen, a side that meant he had been in the military or was trained in the martial arts.

As the days went by, we started getting used to him and one morning, he asked me and my brother what our dad did for a living. I told him he was an airline pilot. Then he told us that he spoke seven languages. Another morning, around 7:30 a.m., I saw him helping a college kid with his physics assignment.

People in the neighborhood felt sorry for him and sent him leftovers to eat. My mom even sent him homemade cakes and he was always very thankful for them. My brother and I noticed that he would never spend the night in the cardboard box, but would show up there in the morning.

One night, we heard some people arguing on our street. We looked out the balcony and saw the Feather Man surrounded by four militia guys. They had grabbed him; one had each of his arms, pulling them tightly behind him while another punched him in the stomach with all his might. Another had a gun pointed to his temple and kept asking him "Where is your radio, where is your radio?" Even though they beat on him for at least fifteen minutes, he didn't give in. He was a very tough guy.

When people started coming up to their balconies and the militia guys noticed everyone was watching, we thought they were going to shoot him, but instead, they let him go.

The next morning, we found out that our neighbor on the second floor, a lady that lived by herself for many years, told the militia that the Feather Man had said something that offended her and so they grabbed him.

The woman had no eyebrows and so she drew them in with heavy, exaggerated lines and wore bright red lipstick. If the Feather Man said something to offend the lady, why were they asking about "his radio"? It all seemed strange.

After that incident, nobody messed with the Feather Man. Then he disappeared for a week and showed up right by the lighthouse at a popular grocery store called Fakouri's. He had on expensive Italian shoes, pressed dress pants, and a nice hat with feathers, nothing like the rough and ragged clothes we were accustomed to seeing him wear. My mother asked him why we hadn't seen him in a while. He looked past her, avoiding her gaze, and said with a mysterious air, "I don't know. Ask the store owner" as he continued to munch on expensive grapes and walk past us out the door.

My mother looked at us, shook her head, and wondered aloud if he was just another mentally ill street person or something more.

# Chapter 19
## The Soccer Field Bombing

There was a shop across from our building called Corner Sport where we hung out a lot. The owner loved kids. He had an African grey parrot that sat in a big cage outside the shop. All the parrot did all day was whistle at the ladies who walked by and say the most vulgar Arabic cuss words that you can imagine, using them perfectly in a sentence as he said them.

He also echoed the mosque calling for prayer saying "Allahu Akbar." He was very loud and very clear with his words as if it were a person speaking. He made us laugh and we could hear him all the way up to the fifth floor as if he were right there beside us.

At night time, the owner would put him inside and in the morning he would put him back out on the sidewalk. The parrot's name was Ahmed. He would also call out to Max, the neighborhood dog, and Max would look around at him.

One day, while talking with Ahmed, the parrot, we started noticing that there was more anti-aircraft fire than usual. So, my mother came to the balcony and called for us. Other moms in other buildings did the same.

After running up the stairs to the fifth floor, we went to the back balcony where we usually sat in our positions waiting for the planes to come by and getting our plant sprayers ready. The anti-aircraft fire started more intensely than we had ever seen before.

As the sound of the jets got closer, the anti-aircraft guns got louder. We saw a jet come by a lot lower this time. It flew over our building and we could barely catch up with our spray guns because it came by with such great speed.

We could hear the anti-aircraft guns firing from the soccer field and within a minute or two we heard a noise from the jets we had never heard before. As long as we had been in the war, we had never heard the screeching noise that the jet made when it started circling over our building, the lighthouse, and the soccer field.

We quickly dropped our plant sprayers because we knew this was different from any other times that jets had flown over. As the anti-aircraft guns kept firing, the jets continued that horrific screeching. We ran to the front balcony because we lost sight of the plane as it had already passed our building.

By the time we got to the front balcony, which was only fifty feet away, we heard the bomb release from the plane. We could hear the whistling of the plane diving and dropping its bomb load. Just hearing that noise made everyone freeze where they were standing.

Then came a shock wave with the loudest explosion we had ever heard. Our whole building shook, all the curtains were blown up and out, our heavy dining room table, which weighed a couple of hundred pounds, moved across the floor as did all the chairs. All the potted plants on the balcony tipped over. We heard the sound of shattering glass and people screaming.

My mom and my brothers' faces were ghostly white because we had never experienced bombs dropping that close to us. I quickly grabbed the emergency bag containing money, important documents, gold, and a gun and ran toward the safest area near the elevator door.

When I grabbed onto the elevator door, we heard more anti-aircraft fire and another bomb being released onto the soccer field. The second shock wave was just as strong as the first one. Our building rocked back and forth and I could feel the pressure change in our ears as the elevator door jerked back and forth from the pressure.

I decided to run down the stairs to the basement bomb shelter. I must have broken a record running because I was the first one to get there. Down there it was dark and I had to wait for my eyes to adjust. My heart was pounding from fear.

Out of the four anti-aircraft guns on the soccer field, only one was still firing. The plane circled another time and, as I was waiting for other people to come down there, three brothers from across the street, refugees living over the coffee shop, came down the stairs into the bomb shelter. They were crying hysterically.

"Why are you crying?" I asked.

One replied, "We have been bombed before in another area where we lived here in Beirut." He then rolled up his sleeves and showed me the burn marks on his arms, burn marks that were the result of phosphorous bombs that had fallen where he lived before.

After they calmed down a little bit, the plane dropped a third bomb and more glass came down. You could hear shattering glass, exploding light bulbs, the breaking of any glass that had not already been broken.

Some Syrian troops ran away from the soccer fields, opened two doors to an underground shelter between a furniture store and Corner Sport, and went in. They were all pale-faced.

Still, that one anti-aircraft gun on the soccer field continued to fire at the plane. The plane circled one more time and dropped the last bomb.

Again, we felt a huge shock wave from the explosion and our ears popped for the fourth time. The pressure from the explosion blew back our shirts and pant legs as if we were standing in a tornado, our heart rates accelerating rapidly.

After that last bomb, there was complete silence. No more firing from the soccer field. Then we heard the noise of the planes fading away in the distance. There was not one sound outside until we started coming out of the bomb shelter.

I walked out in front of the building, but stayed under the overhang of the balconies just in case the planes returned. I could see all the glass from the coffee shop was broken and lying on the sidewalk. To my left under our building was a pharmacy and to the right was an eyeglass store. The shop grates were drawn down but the windows behind them were shattered.

I started seeing the Syrian soldiers emerging from the bomb shelter nearby. One of the neighbors across the street yelled, "Did they just hit the soccer fields?" I looked up toward the soccer fields, which were hidden from me by buildings, and saw plumes of smoke rising in the sky.

Knowing that's what they were targeting gave me some sense of relief. I ran back up the stairs with the emergency bag and saw my mom, Dani, and Wess still by the elevator. I told them that the Israeli jets had hit the anti-aircraft guns on the soccer field which was their intended target. As everyone calmed down, you could hear people scooping up glass and quiet whisperings because we were all still in shock.

I went downstairs later that afternoon because I wanted to see what happened at the soccer field. I used the excuse that I wanted to check on our car, but instead ran with Omar down the street towards the lighthouse.

Because the lighthouse sits on the highest point, we were able to look down over the soccer field. You could see big holes there, big enough to hold a VW bug. Jet black smoke was coming out of them. One of the craters was on the boardwalk beside the soccer field right in the middle of two old palm trees that were still burning. Red dust was blowing in the air from the clay of the soccer field.

The Syrian soldiers had closed all access to the soccer field and were removing the dead and evacuating the injured. You could see the sandbags for protecting the anti-aircraft guns were blown apart and the guns were twisted from the force of the explosions, not from a direct hit.

We asked one of the soldiers before heading home what had happened to that last anti-aircraft gun because we could not see it from where we were. He said that it had been hit. That soldier was the only one who continued to fire at the planes unlike the rest who took off running.

As we headed home, neighbors would ask, "What did you see, what did you see?" We told them that the soccer field had been hit and no one would be allowed to get any closer to it than we did.

I got home and told my mom and Wess what had happened. My mom asked, "Did you go down there?"

"No," I said, "someone told me."

# Chapter 20
## PLO Begins Evacuation and Father Returns a Second Time

A week after the planes bombed us, the Palestinians, the Israelis, and the Lebanese government agreed on a major ceasefire. The Palestinians agreed to move out of Lebanon although the majority of them wanted to stay and fight. Even the female PLO fighters wanted to stay.

Now that there was a ceasefire and an agreement that the Palestinians would leave, more aid from the UN in the way of food and supplies started coming to the city. People began cleaning up the streets, but there was still no electricity or trash pickup, so the burning of the trash continued. Israeli checkpoints around the city started to let people, mainly women and children, come in and out through them.

For a second time, we saw a yellow cab coming down the street. It was my dad returning once again. We ran down the stairs to help him with his bags. He was shocked at the piles of debris stacked up and he was devastated when he saw Nasser's, his friend's restaurant, completely wiped off the street. Some buildings were not even recognizable.

After hugging and kissing him, we told him that he had once again missed some really exciting stuff. We continued to tell him about the planes dropping bombs at the soccer fields. But our main concern was what was in those suitcases for us.

He was amazed at how strong we were as we were able to carry those heavy suitcases up five flights of stairs. He was greeted by the

Syrian concierge of our building who also told him about all he had missed while he was gone. You could tell my dad was affected by the way we had been living with no electricity, no running water, and having to light the nights with candles and kerosene lanterns. He would be startled every time there was gunfire, which was every few minutes, while we continued to put puzzles together on the dining room table while he was heading toward the door. We told him not to be scared and that it was a normal, everyday thing.

He wanted to know how his mother was doing, but we did not want to risk taking the car there because there might be a break in the ceasefire, which had happened a few times. It was a ten minute run or, if my dad was along, a fifteen minute walk to my grandmother's. So, we set off for her home and were happy to see that she and my uncles were still alive, something we could only find out by visiting because there were no working phones or other means of communication.

Around 3:00 that afternoon, we heard the sounds of gunboats firing in our general direction. We had been playing cards outside my grandmother's house near that vegetable garden that fed us during the war.

Jumping up, we knocked the table over, spraying cards across the grass, and ran into my grandmother's house. Teta looked up at us with a confused expression, and then one of the bombs hit a lot closer. Then she knew.

My father grabbed her by the arm and took her to the back rooms where all the windows were barricaded with sandbags. After some of the shells landed nearby, we could hear shrapnel bouncing off the building and then pinging off the telephone pole. Ten minutes later, it was complete silence again.

Everyone started slowly looking around before emerging from the houses. My uncle told us to stay inside a little longer while he looked around outside. He pointed out two pieces of fresh, silvery shrapnel and the trails of sand where they had punctured the sandbag.

We found out that across the street the building owned by my dad and uncles had a skid mark on the roof where one of the shells slid across it, hit the metal post holding up the grapevines, veered away from my grandmother's house, and landed in the cushion of a four-seat swing set in the yard. It didn't explode and was later carried away by some Palestinian fighters. We were so lucky that the bomb ricocheted away from us thanks to that metal grapevine post.

After a few more ceasefires, the Palestinians started getting ready to leave the city. They began leaving in convoys of trucks and jeeps, carrying only their light weapons with them while leaving behind heavy artillery. We watched as the convoys headed along the coastline boardwalk to the freight ships that would take them away.

The Palestinians were saluted as heroes by the most of the Lebanese in West Beirut as the convoys left. Each day a small convoy would drive down the coast on its way to the ships. People shot automatic weapons up in the air as a salute to them for defending the city. All the buildings with windows had people on balconies and as the convoy got closer, the shooting got louder. Thousands of anti-tank rockets were fired into the air. There were so many guns being fired that you could not hear yourself speak.

All day on the radio, announcements were made trying to discourage people from shooting in the air because a few people died from the shots as they rained down, both in the Palestinian and the civilian population. But, nobody listened and the shooting continued.

One morning at my grandmother's, we began celebrating that the war was going to be over. When the convoy got closer, my dad decided to take part in the celebration as the shooting got closer and louder.

He ran inside my grandmother's house with his garden clothes on and came out with an AK-47 and a fully loaded magazine. He told us to step behind him under the covering of a balcony. He cocked the weapon back making a distinctive noise that unfortunately we were all familiar with. He clicked the lever on full automatic and proceeded to fire in the air.

We were both scared and excited at the same time. My other uncles did the same from their balconies. As he emptied the thirty-round clip into the air, he asked me to go inside to get his chest vest that held six magazines in six separate pockets.

I brought it back to him and began handing him one magazine after the other. Because he was shooting in full automatic, you could see all the shell casings spraying out the side of the gun at a fast clip and landing into an open area next to the balcony.

My little brother Dani ran out unexpectedly to grab one of the shell casings. He picked it up and after a second, he dropped it and started crying because it was still scorching hot. There was no ice to give him so he had to tough it out. Even that didn't stop us from continuing the shooting.

After the convoy passed, other areas started shooting. It was as if they were doing the "wave" in a coliseum. This went on for about a week. There were some days when my brother and I put a recorder out on the balcony just to record the gunfire.

After the Palestinians evacuated the city, the convoys moved toward the port where they were loaded onto ships. The Druze militia leader,

Walid Jumblat, went to the port with the last convoy and proceeded to pull out his gun and shoot in the air as a salute to the Palestinians. Now all was quiet since there was no more fighting. The city held its breath and waited for the Israelis to invade.

# Chapter 21
## Israeli Tanks on the Streets of Beirut

Before the Israelis entered the city, the roads were open and that is when my dad had to go back to work. Because Beirut International Airport was closed, he took a cab from Beirut to Damascus, Syria, and flew out from there.

A lot of people were scared of what Israel would do when they came into the city. Almost all families in Beirut had guns, but now there were even more because the Palestinians gave away their guns as they left the city. The Murabitoon, a Sunni militia, had inherited enough Palestinian guns to defend the entire city.

Citizens began burying their weapons in the ground or tossing them off balconies into gardens because they feared Israel would come searching for weapons. In my grandmother's garden, which was surrounded by tall buildings, my uncles, cousins, and I found bullets, fully-loaded magazines, grenades, and belts of ammunition which we added to our collection.

Many people used huge inner tubes from truck tires to hide their weapons. They first greased the weapons and the bullets to keep out moisture and then stuffed them inside the inner tube, sealed it tight, and buried it. The grease kept the guns and ammo from getting rusted.

One man, next to my grandmother's house, took his time with a chisel and carved out a section of concrete wall, put his gun into a plastic bag, stuffed it in the hole, patched the hole with concrete, and painted it. Later, when the Israelis came looking for weapons, he and his son were standing outside near the concrete wall. When asked by the Israelis, the dad replied that he had no weapons.

They took the son away from the dad, gave him some candy, and asked him if he had seen his dad put any weapons away. The son pointed to the wall where his dad had the gun hidden. The Israelis dug the gun and the ammunition out and then beat the boy's father, kicking him, punching him, and using the butts of their guns on him for lying.

After they left, the father recovered and started beating his son. You could hear the son screaming while the dad kept beating him and beating him until some of the neighbors ran down and separated him from his son who was only five years old.

A few days before the Israelis started moving into Beirut, my mother decided to sign me up at ACS to take more English tutoring with one of my soon-to-be teachers for the upcoming fall session. Since we figured the war was going to be over, I might as well, she thought, get a few classes in.

After only a few sessions with the tutor, my mother showed up at ACS unexpectedly one day. I was surprised to see her there because I usually walked to and from school. She said we needed to leave right away because the Israeli army was entering the city.

The thought of seeing a full-fledged Israeli army with all its gear, guns, and tanks was both exciting and frightening to me. I hopped into our VW bug, my mom popping a wheelie as we started the drive home, carefully taking shortcuts and veering away from the beach area which was still closed because of mines. That ride was like being in a NASCAR race. Since there were no seatbelts in the car, she would throw her arm across me every time she took a sharp turn or slammed on the brakes.

We were the only car on the road. It only took us a few minutes to get home. Everybody on our street was on the balconies listening to their hand-held radios which were announcing that the Israeli army had started to enter the city. When we got into our building, we started to hear a few gunshots followed by small-arms fire and a few rocket-propelled grenades. Then, it would start again, coming from different directions and then a long pause.

About 10:00 in the morning, we started to hear Israeli tanks rolling by the American University of Beirut and advancing toward the Saudi Arabian Embassy. The closer they got, the more vibrations there were and the clearer the noise of the armored personnel carriers and tanks.

When they stopped in front of the Saudi Embassy, we could only see the lead car, a Jeep. The commander came out with maps in his hands and, using a loud speaker, he called down our street for the mayor. The mayor came out, walked up the street towards him and they started to talk. The commander gestured toward the door of the Concorde Hotel where they stayed for about twenty minutes.

When the mayor emerged from the Hotel with the commander close behind him, he walked quickly back to his coffee shop across the street. The jeep then pulled up in our street, the tanks slowly following from behind the building. Huge plumes of diesel smoke rose above them as they took a hard left onto our street.

My two brothers and I, like all our neighbors, watched from the balcony as they rolled slowly down the street. The tanks were green with long antennas reaching high up above them, two tanks following behind the first one. As they got under our building, you could feel the vibrations and hear the dishes rattling in our china cabinet. The bulky tanks tried to squeeze by the cars parked on the narrow streets, slicing off the front and rear bumpers of each one as they slowly rolled by.

One of the Israeli soldiers sitting on top of the lead tank behind a fifty-caliber machine gun held a magazine out in front of him as if he were reading, appearing calm and cool, but he was really keeping his eyes on the buildings, the street, and all surrounding areas.

Once all three tanks were on our street, they stopped while foot soldiers ran along each side of the street with their guns drawn. They had been hiding behind the concrete walls and entrances of our buildings. As soon as I saw them, I ran inside and got our camera. From my perch, I took a picture of four Israeli soldiers running together down our street with their guns drawn.

When the last tank stopped, a jeep with a high ranking Israeli officer and two soldiers pulled in right behind it. The jeep stopped near the Feather Man's make-shift cardboard house.

When the Feather Man crawled out and stood up, the officer jumped out of the jeep, saluted him, and handed him his Israeli Colonel's uniform. Everyone's jaws dropped as they watched, even the ones who suspected him all along of being a spy, even a Syrian spy as there were many around.

But, instead, he was an Israeli Colonel sent to check out the area in preparation for the invasion of Beirut. He saluted the officer handing him his shirt, pulled it on over his ragged clothing, and climbed into the jeep as the driver began to turn the jeep around.

Now it all made sense. The fighting techniques used on the kids who tried to steal his feather stick were from military training and his ability to speak seven languages and work complicated physics problems showed he was highly educated. He befriended the people in our neighborhood to learn as much as he could about them and the street where they lived in preparation for the invasion. And now he was being lauded by his own as a hero as he headed by jeep to a nearby Israeli command post.

After ten minutes in our street, the tanks began to move further down. Once they got to the bottom of our street, someone opened fire at the Israeli tank from behind a car. In a split second, the Israeli tank swung its turret and fired without discrimination. The round hit the movie theater which then went up in flames. After that, we did not hear any more gunshots. The smoke from the theater was heavy and black. When the wind blew in our direction, you could smell the awful odor of the foam seats burning inside the theater, a smell that lingered for days.

After the tanks passed through our street, we heard some more gunfire and rocket-propelled grenade explosions coming from Al Hamra Street but, thankfully, within fifteen to twenty minutes it was quiet again.

Late that afternoon, the Israeli Army took positions in a building farther down the street from us about five hundred feet away from the lighthouse, something we discovered when we sneaked away to the lighthouse to play.

An Israeli soldier asked my brother Wess to help him back up an army truck. Wess agreed and stood behind the truck waving at the soldier to tell him how far to back up and when to stop. The soldier gave him gum and candy for helping him. Of course, I never saw any of the gum or candy.

The news radio started to announce that the Israeli soldiers were coming into the neighborhood with big open trucks to collect weapons. It was at that point that everyone began tossing weapons into gardens from their balconies or burying them.

A large truck pulled onto our street with a jeep following it, a loud speaker announcing that whoever had weapons should bring them down and throw them in the back of the truck or they would come door to door looking for them.

My mother had buried our gun in one of the flower pots on our balcony. When I asked her where the gun was, she pointed to the flower pot and then placed her finger across her lips meaning "don't tell anyone."

"Let them come and look," I said. "They will never find it."

We watched from our balcony while the gun searches were unfolding. People came down from the buildings carrying guns and ammunition. The soldiers took them, tossing them into the back of the truck which was already loaded with machine guns and ammunition from other neighborhoods. My brother and I had never seen such a large pile of machine guns.

The next day, after the guns had been confiscated, we heard that Tarzi's, the famous ice cream shop across the street from the entrance to the American University of Beirut and the International College of Beirut, was reopening.

Although I ran there as fast as I could, there was already a long line of customers waiting to place their orders. There was a small stairwell that went down to the basement where the ice cream ingredients were prepared and then brought up in five gallon buckets and poured into the machines. To my surprise, the buckets coming up the stairwell were covered in flies. While it didn't seem to faze the person carrying the buckets as he dumped the contents into the machine or the people who were standing in line, I was sickened by it and turned away.

As I walked away, I noticed there was an Israeli soldier standing right across the street. We could hear a commotion between him and five Palestinian kids who appeared to be between the ages of ten and fifteen, three brothers and two sisters, barefooted and very dirty.

They were trying to carry some water across the street. I knew they were Palestinians because of their beautiful dark olive complexions and curly black hair.

I walked towards them to see what was going on when the Israeli soldier, his gun pointed at them, ordered them to put the water buckets down on the ground. He told them to walk away.

As they were walking away, I walked between the kids and the soldier and told him in English that I was an American citizen and these poor people just needed water to drink.

As soon as I started to reach into my back pocket to pull out my American passport, he shoved the bottom of his boot into my chest making me fall backwards over the water buckets, spilling water all over the ground. It knocked the wind out of me and as I got up from the puddle, he said that he didn't see any Americans around.

I started to walk away with the five kids, the sisters crying and thanking me for taking up for them. I told the little girl that I was the one that should be crying, not her.

I walked about five car lengths away from the solider, turned around, gave him the finger, and called him some dirty names in Arabic and ran home.

Once I got home, I took my shirt off, went to the bathroom and used the bucket of water from the bathtub to get the boot print off before I threw it in the laundry basket. I never wore that shirt again, but kept it hidden in a drawer, a reminder of the hate the Israelis had not only towards the Palestinians, but also towards the Lebanese.

**Picture taken by the author from his fifth floor
balcony of armed Israeli soldiers
entering his street.**

# Chapter 22
## Massacres at Sabra and Shatila Refugee Camps

On the morning of September 16, 1982, we began to hear small-arms fire in the distance that continued for three days. We thought that there were still pockets of resistance, but we never heard any of the usual loud explosions, only small-arms fire.

Three days after the gunfire stopped, there was a major announcement on the radio as well as headlines on the newspaper's front page. There had been massacres at the Palestinian refugee camps of Sabra and Shatila.

The Israelis, who were in control of all of Beirut, allowed the Christian Phalangist militia to enter the refugee camps and shoot all its occupants, some of whom were not Palestinian, but Lebanese.

Since all the Palestinian fighters had left the city, there was no one to defend the refugee families living there. In plain view of the Israelis, the Phalangists shot all the women, children, and the elderly.

Later, we saw in Time magazine the blood-stained walls where they had been lined up and shot. Not one had a gun in his hand. We heard of only two escaping, a thirteen year-old boy and an elderly man.

The newspapers also had pictures of the clean-up after the Phalangists had left. Bulldozers were brought in and all the bodies numbering in the hundreds or thousands, depending upon the source, were wrapped in white sheets while mass graves were dug. Lime was thrown into the pits where the bodies were then dumped. It was shocking to us that the Israelis did nothing to stop the massacre.

After a few weeks of the Israeli army occupying the city, resistance fighters did a drive-by on Al Hamra Street, opening fire at a coffee shop killing a high-ranking Israeli officer and some soldiers that were with him. Many similar actions were taken against the Israelis in an attempt to make them leave.

The Israeli Army did not leave Beirut, however, until May of 1983 after the bombing of the U.S. Embassy in April and before the Marine barracks bombing in October.

Of course, there was no celebration for the Israelis as they left the city. But, as a parting gift to the citizens of Beirut, an Israeli army bulldozer shoved all of the illegal make-shift shops that were along the boardwalk facing Pigeon Rock on Raouche Street into the Mediterranean Sea.

# Chapter 23
## Disneyland, Beirut-Style

With the Israeli army gone, the airport reopened and flights began to come back in. Some of the Lebanese Army started to patrol the city. A lot of Embassy personnel, Americans and people who had left because of the Israeli invasion, came back, my dad among them.

My dad took us sightseeing in his car, the sights being the devastation and destruction of our once beautiful Beirut. Before that, we had not been allowed to go more than a few blocks from where we lived. After they cleared all the obstacles and land mines from the beachfront roads, our first destination was the area where the Nasser Restaurant had been.

It was in ruins and all the buildings along the way were flattened. Today, T.G.I. Friday's, a chain restaurant, occupies the space where the Nasser once stood.

While driving, we had to be careful to dodge the bomb craters which could easily swallow up our small car. The debris and shards of broken glass were spread throughout the whole city. Everywhere you turned, more glass, more debris, and more skeletons of cars.

The soccer field was used to dump all the used military equipment which included anti-aircraft guns, tanks, armored personnel carriers, and rocket launcher trucks. To my friends and me, it was like having our own personal amusement park.

Taking all the kids on our street with us, we ran past the tennis courts toward the soccer field, the closest thing to Disneyland that we would ever see.

Now here lay all the weapons and tanks which we always heard and saw but could never touch or go inside. We climbed into the tanks and, like little rats, stuck our heads out of the holes. Some of the tanks had their treads all destroyed, but we didn't care.

We found helmets inside the tanks, put them on, and acted as if we were shooting, looking through the scopes and making firing noises.

Then, one of my cousins found an anti-aircraft gun that appeared to be in better shape than the rest of the stuff. Jumping off the tanks, we ran towards him through an obstacle course created by metal, shards of glass, and debris.

Three of us took positions on the anti-aircraft gun. One was the guy who aimed, one was the guy who used the lever to rotate the gun, and one was the guy who pressed the pedal to make the gun fire. Now we could play war for real and for the next couple of weeks, it was our playground.

Right before school started, trucks came through the soccer field and hauled all the tanks away. Disneyland was closed and school was opening. Needless to say, my friends and I were disappointed by both.

The whole city started to come alive again. Shops began to open and you could tell things were getting better because you could hear cars honking everywhere.

We decided one afternoon to have our last soccer game before school started in front of the Corner Sport shop on our street. We put two rocks at each end as goals and Omar brought out his old soccer ball, the one stuffed with newspapers.

While waiting for cars to pass so we could continue our game, we heard the loud screeching of an Israeli jet as if it were going to drop a bomb on us and everybody hit the ground. The owner of Corner Sport came out doubled over in laughter because it was Ahmed, the parrot, who made that screeching jet noise sound so real that our hearts were pounding and our faces were pale in fear as we picked ourselves up off the street.

One of the kids started cussing at the parrot for scaring us. Ahmed just cussed back at him. His impression of the Israeli jet was perfect!

One late afternoon, another good thing happened: the electricity came on all of a sudden and the whole neighborhood started cheering as if someone had scored a goal. We went to grab our Atari game which had not been used in three or four months, but before we plugged in the game, we decided to ride the elevators because everything was a new toy once the power was on.

Once we sat down and plugged the game up, we only had about five minutes to play when the lights went back out. You could hear everybody cussing and calling the government names.

The power going off and on caused many problems. A friend of ours at the German Institute located by the lighthouse in Ras Beirut, was beaten by his parents because the power came on unexpectedly one evening.

Three months earlier, when the power was on, he had invited us over to watch a dirty movie and, as soon as he put the movie in the VCR, the power went off.

Three months later, while his family had some guests over for dinner, the electricity came back on and the movie started playing. His parents were embarrassed and shocked in front of their friends and proceeded to beat his butt.

He didn't think it was funny, but the rest of us could not stop laughing when we heard what had happened.

# Chapter 24
## UN Peacekeepers Arrive
## Embassy and Marine Barracks Bombed

Around the time school started, we learned that the UN was sending a peacekeeping force into Lebanon. The U. S. Marines, part of that force, were positioned in barracks close to the airport. We had no idea at the time of what was to come because of the UN's presence. But, thankfully, life seemed to be returning to normal.

I was happy to go back to school because we had been isolated from people. It was good to make new friends. Most of the children there were from different countries, children of diplomats, embassy employees, or Americans like me. The whole city started coming back to life. Shops began opening again and the cleanup of rubble and debris was underway except for some of the big buildings that were heavily damaged. A lot of unexploded ordinance were found and destroyed. And some just exploded on their own.

Some of the ammunition and weapons abandoned in my grandmother's garden exploded accidentally one day when my father decided to burn a pile of brush and clippings from the garden. He dumped gasoline over the pile of brush unaware the ammo was there. He realized that he did not have any matches with him so he ran up to my grandmother's house, got the matches, and returned. He took a small rag, lit it, and tossed it toward the brush. Before the burning rag could reach the pile of brush, there was a huge explosion from the fumes given off by the evaporating gasoline. It shook the whole neighborhood. A couple of my aunts, who were on the balconies watching, screamed and ran inside.

A few minutes later as the fire was growing stronger, unexploded rounds started to go off. For about two hours, the bullets rang into the sky in all directions until the fire finally went out. After that, there was no more burning of anything.

After four months of school and having a normal life, the electricity began to come on more frequently, staying on for around five hours a day. We started going to friends' parties and to the beach. The school was at full capacity.

One day, my friend Salem and I were coming back from our lunch break at the local sandwich shop where there was a pinball machine we loved to play. It was only a few hundred feet from our school. It was cloudy that day and there was a light drizzle of rain falling. We heard a light rumble which sounded like thunder so we didn't pay any attention to it.

Ten minutes later the janitor told us that the American Embassy had just been blown up. Immediately, Salem and I ran straight down to the beach. When we got to the boardwalk, we made a right and ran a mile all the way to the Embassy.

As we were running, we could hear sirens from behind us. When we arrived at the scene, we were out of breath. There were chunks of concrete all over the road before we got to the building. There were Lebanese Army soldiers looking down into the water. We leaned over the railings and saw what they were looking at. It was an armored personnel carrier belonging to the Lebanese Army that had been guarding the embassy.

Apparently, the driver panicked after the explosion and somehow ran the armored personnel carrier off the boardwalk and onto the rocks, about ten feet down. Some of the guards that came out of the carrier were crying and one was holding his hand to his head, blood running down his face. At least none of them died.

When we looked at the American Embassy, half of it had fallen. There was smoke and debris everywhere. In the middle of the Embassy there had been a little garden where a German Shepherd dog ran around. Now there was only rubble.

My aunt's house was directly behind the embassy, but they only had their windows blown out. No one was hurt. More army people started showing up on the scene as well as trucks full of U.S. Marines. I picked up a piece of glass that was from the embassy, glass that had wires embedded in it to hold it together in an explosion.

The Lebanese Army and the U.S. Marines ordered everybody out and sealed off the whole area. We could see helicopters coming in from the Mediterranean and landing on the boardwalk with equipment, cadaver dogs, and searchlights so they could dig for the remains of the people in the Embassy. Salem and I had to go back to school and grab our book bags as all the students were told to go home.

For the next few days, the digging for bodies continued day and night. It was the talk at school since most of the kids were American. Someone drove by the boardwalk a few blocks away from the embassy and fired a few rounds at the Marines and drove off. The Marines became more alert, placing more security around the Embassy.

I asked one of the Marines what they were doing in Lebanon. He said they were on a peace mission. I asked him where all his ammunition and guns were. He said they only issued them three rounds apiece.

Then, he asked me if I could get him some hashish. I told him for $10 I could look into it. I asked him where he was going to be the next few days. He said either here until this mess is cleaned up or at the Marine barracks by the airport.

As I was walking away, I turned around and said, "Only three bullets in your gun? You came all the way to Beirut, Lebanon, with only three rounds? Even small children here have more than that." He smiled at me and I walked away.

It took a week or two to get all the bodies out of the Embassy rubble. Afterwards, there was a little more tension in the city, but daily life still appeared to be somewhat normal. I was going to tutoring after school three times a week for English and twice a week at home for math since I was having problems concentrating.

One October morning around 6:00 a.m., we heard a huge explosion. All the buildings around us shook and some people reported that chunks of concrete landed in their streets or in their neighborhoods.

A few months of quiet and now this, again. Turning on the radios, we heard there had been an explosion close to the airport, five miles from us. A few minutes later more news bulletins were issued saying that the Marine barracks had been hit by a suicide bomber and the whole place was leveled. Immediately after that, helicopters from American aircraft carriers in the Mediterranean began arriving to help recover the 241 dead U.S. servicemen from the barracks. I wondered if the young marine I had met outside the Embassy was among them.

The tension grew in the city since this was a large scale attack on the U.S. forces. The Lebanese Army set up even more checkpoints and drove into neighborhoods and detained people.

One who was detained lived on our street. They came one day and took Omar's dad away along with a few others in our neighborhood. Other neighborhoods were experiencing the same kind of treatment with some being physically beaten.

At the time Amin Gemayel was the president of Lebanon. We felt unsafe because the army was supposed to protect us, but what we saw was frightening. We noticed in some areas sandbags and barriers were being erected. This was the beginning of the revolt of the people against the Lebanese Army.

# Chapter 25
## Lebanese Army Fights West Beirut Militias

One late afternoon before the last class period at school, Salem and I were entering the school building. As soon as we opened up the big steel door, we heard muffled pops from a distance followed by huge explosions around the school.

We ran into the school building and up to the second floor where my math class met. When we entered the classroom, everybody was on the floor, including a Sikh student, his turbaned head tucked under the desk, crying. As more shells landed around the school, panic erupted and people did not know in which direction to run. I leaned down to the Indian student as he was crying and said, "Welcome to Lebanon. What else did you expect?"

The shells started to get closer and sounded much louder than ones we had heard before. I ran down the stairwell to get to the front of the building, dodging kids and teachers who appeared panicked, not knowing which way to go.

Looking outside the front of the building, I saw people running in all directions and heard cars honking non-stop. The bombs were coming in such close intervals that I didn't want to take the chance of running home.

Instead, I ran across the street to the School Administration Building, which also housed students. A loud shell exploded in the bus lot of the International College of Beirut, across the street from us. It hit one of the buses causing a chain reaction with one burning bus torching another, causing even more panic.

A friend of mine, Christian, whose grandparents owned Tokyo Restaurant, asked me as he ran past if I was going to go home because we sometimes used the same shortcut.

"No," I said," go ahead. I want to wait it out."

As he ran, more shells came in and we could smell smoke from the burning buses. The teachers seemed paralyzed by fear, crying and unable to regain composure. I thought to myself that they must have missed the Israeli invasion as this all seemed so new to them.

I was able to ask one secretary who lived on our street to let my parents know I was going to stay at the school for now. I saw my friend Salem who asked me if I wanted to go home with him since he lived inside the University of Beirut campus, directly across from our school.

We ran the half-block to the campus. There was a Lebanese Army guard standing at the gate and usually they stop and ask where you are going, but you could see that he was distracted and scared. We ran right past him and went to the sixth floor of Salem's building.

From his balcony you could see the whole seaport and East Beirut. We heard more pops and started seeing splashes into the sea where the ships in the port were being targeted by militias in the mountains firing into the sea. After a few shells landed next to the ships, the ships headed full speed back out into the Mediterranean, a trail of sporadic shells landing near or around them.

The Marines, who were still at the boardwalk, closed the boardwalk area down and hid behind the sandbagged positions they had built. As the sun went down, more shells landed around us with horrific explosions that shook everything. Since the shelling was constant with no break, we knew this was serious. It seemed to be mainly our area, Ras Beirut, which was being targeted. All night we could hear the whooshing noise of shells flying over the campus and landing close by. Our school library was hit and shells landing in the street caused cars to flip over on their backs from the pressure of the explosions.

Salem's mother brought us some blankets, which we paid no attention to, concentrating instead on whether we were going to make it or not since the shells kept getting closer and closer. It was like we were sitting in a submarine waiting for the depth charge to hit. As each got closer, we feared the next would be the one to hit us. The explosions were so great I began to doubt that the building we were in could protect us any longer.

All night the shells kept landing in the same area and we could smell fires burning. Even though we had electricity from the campus generators, the power blinked several times. The shells were getting so close that I thought to myself that this time I might not make it. The only thing I kept thinking about was that if I did die, I would get to see my grandmother. After that, I wasn't scared anymore.

Then I kept wondering why they would bomb so close to us since there was no military facility next to our school. It was mainly a populated civilian area with schools and homes. It was indiscriminate bombing. The smell of smoke kept getting stronger and stronger and the shells were coming in threes. I knew some of them had landed in the school because the building we were in across the street from the school shook violently.

At about 4:00 in the morning, the bombing stopped. All we heard was sporadic small-arms fire and a few explosions, but nothing like the shelling. At 8:00 a.m., when it seemed that things had quieted down, I told Salem and his mother that maybe it was time for me to run across to the school and see what I could do about getting home. I went down to the campus gate where a Lebanese guard stood with his M-16 resting against a wall a good ways from him. He was very nervous, he was crying, and he didn't care who went in or out of the gate.

I couldn't cross the street at the moment but had to wait until the Marines down the beach waved to me that it was clear to run. I had to run quickly through the alley between the two schools. With my backpack, I ran across the street.

I asked the person standing there why the army guy was crying. He said that he was Christian and realized that if his Lebanese Army was doing all the shelling and had not been able to occupy West Beirut, things would be difficult for him because he was on the wrong side of the line. His army was unable to take over West Beirut, a Moslem and Druze section, and he could be in danger. I knew that they probably wouldn't hurt him, but they definitely would take his M-16.

The look on the faces of the people when I walked into the school was like a scene from a horror movie. Everyone looked terrified and as if they hadn't slept in a week. I could still smell smoke and as I entered the student lounge towards the administration office, I saw that the courtyard in the center was completely devastated by a shell that landed in its middle. It had dug out a huge hole in the concrete.

A few feet away where my tutor lived with his wife and cat, a huge shell had landed right in the middle of their apartment. The hole was ten feet wide and fifteen feet deep. His apartment was destroyed and his cat was missing.

All the kids and teachers were lined up in the hallway where they apparently spent the night. We could still hear some small-arms fire, but after all the shelling we had endured the night before, nobody paid much attention to it. Everybody was happy to be alive, congratulating each other on surviving the shelling.

My tutor kept looking at his house, kept crying and wiping his tears with his wife next to him, saying how lucky they were that they decided to go to the administration building instead of staying in their apartment. It had been a direct hit, taking down one side of his apartment and seriously damaging the other apartments.

All the windows were blown out within a five hundred foot radius. Later we heard that the U. S. Marines, who along with the Lebanese Army, were responsible for the shelling had apologized to the tutor for the loss of his home and the significant damage done to our school.

I had entered the building from the back entrance, walking through toward the front door to see what the real damage was. I took five steps and hadn't even gotten to the gate when I could see a huge hole in the school library across the street.

Looking down to the street, I saw that it was beyond recognition. The road in front of my school was completely plowed by shells, gaping holes appearing every fifteen feet. All the power lines were down, cables dangling everywhere. A string of cars along the street were completely flipped over and burned to a crisp. Even the cars that were not hit directly had severe damage done to them. I had to stop and look again because it was hard to recognize how things could change that dramatically in twelve hours.

There was a ticking noise coming from the hot cars that had been burning all night as they were beginning to cool down. I was still in shock when out of nowhere my dad pulled up in a Druze militia army jeep with four other armed men, all with smiles on their faces. They pulled in front of the school and my dad hopped out of the jeep and gave me a hug, congratulating me for surviving.

When I told him he should see all the devastation as we were getting into the jeep, he said to me "You haven't seen anything yet." He also said that if it wasn't for our cousins that all of us at the school would have been killed by now.

"What are you talking about?" I asked.

He said that the military base on the boardwalk across from his mother's house was the Lebanese Army strong point from which they were trying to take over the city. He told me that my uncle and my cousins prevented them from crossing the boardwalk by shooting at them from the surrounding buildings overlooking the Army Base.

On hearing that, I shook the hands of the guys in the jeep as I climbed in the back while checking out the AK-47s and all the ammo that was stuck in between the seats. As we drove off, I waved at the people behind me who looked puzzled to see me riding away in a jeep. I signaled to them that I was okay.

We had to drive slowly to avoid skeletons of cars, glass, and big chunks of concrete that covered the road. There were a few of what used-to-be dogs on the sidewalk. They looked like they had been burned while hiding under the cars and the only way I could recognize that they were dogs was because their tails were still intact.

The road turned up a steep incline close to those stairs between the Saudi Embassy and where the building collapsed, those stairs that were my shortcut home. One building that was still under construction had a Lebanese Army personnel carrier the Druze militia had confiscated parked in front of it. The militia member, who was manning the fifty-caliber machine gun, gave us a victory sign as we drove by slowly checking out all the damage.

When we returned his victory sign, he pointed the fifty-caliber machine gun in the sky and fired a few rounds. When we got to the top of the street, we could see all the school busses that had been hit the day before. They were mere metal skeletons, still smoldering.

My dad told the driver to pull over and let us out. We would walk home from there. They insisted that they would take us all the way, but we wanted to stop by and see our uncles' stores which were only four blocks from our house.

Uncle Chiclet and Uncle Hussein were standing outside their burning stores and both were sobbing. They were standing a couple of hundred feet from the stores to avoid possibly exploding propane tanks inside the store. They kept trying to walk into the stores to get their money from the cash registers. But, each time they pulled back because things were still exploding inside. The street would have been unrecognizable if it weren't for their two stores.

The building on the corner across from the police station, a small private school that I had once attended, was damaged beyond recognition. It had been hit by at least six shells, but it looked like a huge wrecking ball had smashed through the building. The strong concrete that I thought could take a lot of damage before falling had been completely smashed in. Not one wall remained straight. All the balconies were ripped off, thick strong balconies. All you could see was rebar where chunks of concrete had been blown out of the building. All the electric lines were down as well as some trees that had been pruned by the shells.

When I started looking around to find something familiar, I noticed that civilian-clothed militia men were everywhere. Some of them had their faces completely covered, but everyone seemed to be happy and they were firing shots in the air. People were driving in the streets, honking, trying to avoid shell holes and chunks of concrete while firing their guns in the air in celebration.

I was really tired and so was everyone around me, but the excitement of all that was going on kept us up. After saying goodbye to my uncles and some of my cousins, we walked home, and as we got closer to the Saudi Embassy, we saw more devastation. We made a left onto our street and I was shocked to see that our street was one of the few that didn't get much damage. The surrounding buildings had shielded us from fire. But, of course, all the glass was blown out of the windows.

Max came running out to us. I petted him, even though he was filthy, because I was happy to see him alive. He followed us down the street to our home. All the neighbors were on their balconies congratulating each other for surviving the worst part of the war that we had experienced, at least the worst so far.

My mom rushed to us as we walked in the door, telling us how the bombs had hit one block over from us but that the buildings across the street, which were hit hard, thankfully shielded our street and our building.

Militia men were driving all through West Beirut celebrating in stolen station wagons. Guns were sticking out of every car window.

As my mom and the neighbors were cleaning the glass fragments from the balconies, my brother Wess and I decided that this was a good time to sneak out of the house. We ran down our street and met our friend Omar. Someone said we should go see the big hole beside the German Embassy, two blocks from my house. We ran and got there within two minutes and saw people standing outside the embassy looking down.

When we got close enough to see, there was a huge hole in the sidewalk about five feet wide and looking down we could see a bomb shelter. The shell had penetrated the sidewalk all the way down to the bomb shelter. Luckily, no one was in it at the time. That showed me that this time the shells that were being used were much stronger than the ones we were accustomed to. That is why there was so much devastation in the city.

We ran back to our street as people shot up into the air and gave us a victory sign. Yes, we were celebrating being survivors even though we were losing our beloved city. Somewhere deep in my soul, I was beginning to question all that I saw and heard.

Those momentary thoughts left me as we ran down to our friend Ali's house overlooking the tennis courts to see how he was. We got around the corner from the lighthouse, where there is usually a big trash pile. One shell had landed in the trash pile, exploded, and exposed the drinking water pipe. There were people using buckets to get some drinking water. It would be a good place to wash our bikes later on, we thought.

Ali was standing outside his house next to someone who looked very familiar. As I got closer, I recognized it was one of my cousins on my dad's side, who at the time belonged to the Druze militia, standing there wearing army green, his AK-47 in one hand and six magazines inside his chest vest. He waved us over. He pointed his gun towards the ocean and emptied a whole clip in the air.

Then he asked us if we wanted to shoot. Intimidated by the gun, we asked him to put it on single shot instead of fully automatic and fired a few shots over the sea. He told us that they fought all night as he pointed to the Lebanese Army base on the beach. We could see it from where we stood. He said that six or seven commandos had been captured and then later released to the Lebanese Army who picked them up by helicopter.

The helicopter made multiple attempts at landing to pick up the wounded and captured. The helicopter would almost touch down and then lift back up out of fear they would be shot at even though the militia told them they would not be fired on.

I wondered if he even realized that I had been in the middle of that firefight, huddled with classmates, waiting out the barrage of fire from both sides.

My cousin said that he and my uncles fought all night from the buildings opposite the army base to prevent the most strategic point of Beirut, Ras Beirut, from being taken over by the Lebanese Army. You could still see holes next to windows in high-rise hotels and buildings where my cousins had been shooting to keep the Lebanese Army from crossing the boardwalk.

The Lebanese Army had Law rocket-propelled grenade launchers made by the U.S. They were very lightweight, could only be used once, and then were thrown away. About three hundred of those launchers were captured by the militias.

My uncle's house was hit by one of those; luckily, the shell hit beside the window and exploded because inside the room were rocket-propelled grenades and ammo boxes stacked against all four inside walls.

They were being used to stop the Lebanese Army from occupying the city. He said that our cousins our age were the magazine loaders. Their job during the intense fighting was to load up magazines and pass them to our other cousin fighters. They ran from building to building carrying large canvas totes of ammo while the fighting was going on.

So the Lebanese Army wouldn't see where all the gunfire was coming from, they had to shoot out a street light that was over their building's entrance. One of my uncles emptied a whole magazine into the light while receiving heavy fire from the Lebanese Army base.

It took all night with the shelling and the shooting for the militias to liberate and capture all the Lebanese Army bases. While we were standing with Ali, he pointed right across from his house where the army had a checkpoint. He said that by morning they were all gone.

So we ran over to their positions, something we could tell by where the sandbags were stacked. We jumped over the sandbags into the small trenches and found no one, only traces of blood and army fatigues that were everywhere. Apparently, when the city fell to the militias, the soldiers took off their recognizable army fatigues and threw them into the trenches.

We thought we were in heaven when we found all those army fatigues. We started trying them on. I put my hand in a fatigue pocket and found some Lebanese money there. We took all the fatigues we could physically carry and gave them to other kids in the neighborhood to put on.

And being kids we came up with the idea to name our neighborhood gang of friends the Zombies. When one of the guys asked why the name Zombies, I told him that we should have been dead so many times before that we were like the walking dead.

We checked on the new tennis courts and only one wall was destroyed, but the building next to it, which was the American Consulate, was heavily damaged. Now the only fighting we could hear was at the Green Line.

Since Beirut was liberated from domination by the Lebanese Army, all the militias that occupied West Beirut started driving to the Green Line to make sure the Phalangists and the Lebanese Army did not cross the Green Line into West Beirut. A section of the Green Line was about two and a half miles from our house, out near the Holiday Inn, where we could still hear sporadic gunfire and a few shells going back and forth. We knew this meant a little time off from school because it would take a while to repair all the damage there.

My brother and I went home to report on all we had seen. My mom wanted us to throw away all the army fatigues, but instead we hid them in the abandoned car by the lighthouse, the same car we had siphoned gas from.

# Chapter 26
## The USS New Jersey

On the night of December 4, 1983, the Marines, who were stationed at the airport using bunkers made from sandbags, were targeted while under the cover of fog. Artillery shells were fired at them from different positions and, because of the fog, it was difficult for the Marines to find the source of the shelling. The artillery barrage had zeroed in on the Marine position, causing injuries and the death of eight Marines. Over the next few months, similar attacks took place. President Reagan was being pressured to pull U.S. forces out of Lebanon and on February 7 he ordered them to withdraw.

On January 9, 1984, prior to their withdrawal, the battleship USS. New Jersey came close to the shore of Lebanon near Beirut. We could see it from our balcony. When it got behind some buildings, my brother Wess and I went up to the rooftop and, as usual, we made our pit stop to water the plants, plants that had turned yellow and were close to death.

Once we got to the rooftop, we could clearly see the battleship New Jersey. It was only a few miles out, the biggest battleship we had ever seen. The sun was just about to set when a huge fiery orange blast emitted from the ship, lighting up the whole city as if it were high noon.

Within seconds we heard the noise of the explosion and all the buildings and glass around us shook. Seconds later we heard a big whooshing noise going over our building. The blast from the battleship was much louder than we anticipated, so we quickly climbed back down the ladder and went back to our flat.

We told our mom and dad what we had seen and my dad got angry with us for being on the roof while this was going on.

A second shell was fired and it took about ten seconds to hear it land. From our balcony, we could only see a part of the ship, the part that was not obstructed from view by the buildings across from us.

A few more rounds were fired after the sun had set making everything glow bright orange. Then, we started counting the seconds it took from hearing the noise until it landed. It took longer than we expected. The targets were Syrian and Druze militia positions.

When it was over, we began hearing reports on our transistor radios about where the shells had landed. One family had reported that the blast where the shells landed was so strong that they could not breathe for ten seconds. The exploding shells caused a major concussion, sucking the air out of the village.

The next day we could see the devastation in the papers as we pulled up our baskets onto the balcony. Those photos showed how bad it had become. Since the civil war and the Israeli invasion, the newspaper had little need for words.

The USS New Jersey firing on Lebanon, January 9, 1984
(Photo by PH1 Ron Garrison, courtesy of
www.history.navy.mil)

# Chapter 27
## Suicide Car Bombs and Assassinations

While the Israelis were out of Beirut, they were still in southern Lebanon. With no tanks or air force or navy, for that matter, Lebanese resistance fighters had to come up with a new way to fight the Israelis.

The best way to pressure the Israeli government was by using suicide car bombers against them. It was hoped that Israeli families whose sons and daughters were in harm's way would pressure their own government to pull out of Lebanon.

Suicide car bombings became the accepted means of resistance and even women became successful at it, taking out Israeli convoys and military installations, and causing heavy casualties to the occupiers. Many other groups joined the effort using their own suicide bombers and every time a successful suicide bombing was broadcast on the radio, everyone celebrated by shooting in the air, a salute to the martyr and the cause for which they died, trying to liberate southern Lebanon from Israeli occupation.

We all felt proud of the resistance since fighting a military powerhouse like Israel seemed impossible. They had air superiority, tanks, navy, and endless supplies of ammunition from the U.S. We felt backed into a corner as we had no electricity, no water, and our land was occupied. We thought we had nothing to lose. Many thought suicide bombing was the last hope and it seemed to be effective as the casualties of the Israeli military were rising and so was pressure from Israeli citizens for the government to get the troops out of Lebanon. Before the suicide bombings, most of the casualties had been on the Lebanese side and now Israel was getting a taste of its own medicine.

The suicide bombers were often interviewed before the bombings. One of them, a beautiful young, well-educated woman, was interviewed before she went on her mission. She made it clear in her interview that she had not been talked into this, that she had not done any drugs, and that she was fully aware of her mission and what it stood for.

When the Israeli military would not let cars into southern Lebanon for fear of more suicide bombers, desperate and determined residents found other ways to fight. An elderly man, who used a donkey instead of a car for his transportation, loaded baskets of explosives across the donkey's back and blew himself and the donkey up at the Israeli checkpoint. Young, old, male, and female had become determined that they would not live under Israeli occupation any longer.

Another young man, who was interviewed by Hezbollah for several days before his mission, seemed very calm and ready to blow himself up for the cause. He had a heavy backpack loaded with explosives and snuck behind enemy lines, detonating himself and causing severe casualties to the Israeli forces and their military compound.

The news traveled quickly all over the world, but especially in Beirut where everyone had small AM-FM transistor radios pressed to their ears. On hearing the news, citizens of Beirut celebrated in their usual fashion, going to the balconies and rooftops and firing their weapons into the air. Rocket-propelled grenades and anti-aircraft guns mounted on the back of pickup trucks fired into the Beirut sky. People soon learned to collect ammunition and have their guns close by, ready for the next announcement, each celebration lasting for about an hour. That happened with each strike on the Israelis and boosted the morale in Lebanon, if only momentarily.

Also, other suicide bombers were filmed as their explosives were detonated against their Israeli targets. This made a bigger impact around the world and showed the amount of devastation a suicide bombing could cause an enemy. These horrible acts of desperation were broadcast all over the Arab world which was supportive of the Lebanese resistance to occupation.

\* \* \*

In January, 1984, when I was back in school, my friends and I visited a café located right next to the school. The place was busy.

While talking to the owner about ordering food, he told me that my dad was there earlier that day asking if I smoked cigarettes. The café was our hangout where we ate, smoked, and played the only pinball machine in the place. I was scared to hear what his reply was to my father when he smiled and said, "Don't worry. I told him you didn't smoke." I was greatly relieved that he didn't tell on me.

A few minutes later while I was waiting to get my order of food, he popped his head from under the counter as he was getting something for someone else and said, "Hey, Sam, guess what they just put on the news?"

I asked, "What?" and he replied in Arabic that the president of American University of Beirut had just been shot.

I said, "What?" Then he repeated it in English.

When the student standing a few feet behind me in line heard what he said, this time in English, he dropped his food on the floor, turned around and started to run, slamming into a steel support beam in the middle of the café. He fell to the ground, got back up, and took off running while pushing everybody out of his way, a look of terror on his face.

As he ran through the door, someone whispered that he was the son of the university president. The owner of the café found out and began apologizing to me that he did not mean to say it for everyone to hear. He did not know that the university president's son was a student standing in line there.

No one knew for sure who had shot him. Most of the students were expected to go to the viewing, but I decided not to go because Americans were being targeted.

# Chapter 28
## Reagan Pulls US Troops from Lebanon

In February, 1984, President Reagan began moving all U.S. troops out of Lebanon. I received a call at the house from someone from the American Embassy saying that all Americans were being evacuated and I was to meet at my school and from there I would be flown by helicopter to the aircraft carrier and brought to the states. I told him I wasn't leaving because my family was still in Beirut. He said if I changed my mind and decided to leave to meet at the American school. When I told my mother, we both shrugged as if to say, "What are we to do?"

I decided to go down to my school after I heard that ninety percent of the students were leaving. I went to Salem's house and he told me they were leaving in the next two days. He gave me lots of his toys: Monopoly, a Slinky, some Army GI Joes, and some trick playing cards, things he could not take with him. I thought it was cool that everybody was giving me their stuff until I realized I would have no one to play these games with. All Americans were evacuated and the population in my school went from a thousand to twenty-eight.

West Beirut became like the "Wild, Wild West." Since we were kids and didn't understand law and order, we thought it was the greatest thing to watch people drive on the wrong side of the road. And, one way streets now went both ways. If you could not pay your landlord, nothing would happen. People could occupy empty apartments whenever they wanted to. If someone had an argument with someone else, they shot it out in the streets. There were so many shootouts in the streets between different militias that a lot of fast-food restaurants and grocery stores stacked sandbags six or seven feet high around the store's perimeter for protection.

It was at that time that I got my first 9 mm handgun from two twelve-year-olds who were shooting it in the parking lot next to the Saudi Embassy. They said they had found it and I gave them fifty Lebanese lira for it. It appeared to be in mint condition. I ejected the magazine and slid the chamber back, clearing out the last round in the gun. I tucked it in my pants, covering it with my baggy shirt and, since I was skinny, you could not see it.

I brought it home and showed it to Wess. Then he told me he had the perfect hiding spot and I, of course, believed him since he always hid everything. We pulled the drawers out of the chest that was built into the wall of our room. We pulled them all out quietly so my mother wouldn't hear.

On the side where the drawers slid in, there was a foot of space. To my surprise, I saw soda cans, candy, and brand new live ammunition all stacked neatly against the wall in that space. We put the gun in there, after I had cleaned it, and quietly slid the drawers back in place. It was the best hiding spot in the whole house, Wess's hiding spot, and now I, too, knew where it was.

Another item that would need hiding was a live hand grenade I got from a friend of mine at school. I shoved it into my pocket and took off for home because I couldn't wait to show it to Wess.

He was sitting on his bed reading one of our comic books when I walked in the room, shut the door behind me, and locked it. Wess looked at me in surprise when he saw me pulling the pineapple-shaped grenade out of my pocket. I sat the grenade on our desk and, when he approached me to get a closer look, I told him I was going to open it to see what was inside.

"What!" he said. "Are you crazy? I wouldn't do that if I were you."

I twisted the top of the grenade which had a spoon-like lever, its safety mechanism, running along its side. This would prevent the grenade from exploding until the lever was released. I unscrewed the grenade and as I did so, my brother Wess backed away saying, "You've lost your mind! You are going to get us all killed."

He jumped behind the bed, holding two pillows over his face and head. In a few seconds, I pulled out the fuse of the grenade and all I could see inside was stuff that looked like black play-dough stuck to the inside walls of the grenade. The fuse in my hand was nothing more than a two-inch copper-looking tube, the detonator. I was told that there were different types of powder in the tube that burned at different rates which gave the grenade a designated time before it exploded. Then, I put it back together by screwing it back on and, as I had been told to do, I put a heavy gauge rubber band around the spoon lever just in case the pin was accidentally pulled.

I added it to our stash of sodas, candy, a gun, and ammunition. Having this stash made us want to go out and get more things to hide away and add to our growing collection.

When school reopened, there was hardly anyone there. I was the only one in my science class with my science teacher Miss Betar. It felt more like being with a tutor all day. At recess, there were only ten or twelve kids in the whole courtyard. I became close with my teachers since I was the lone student in some of the classes, all the other Americans having been evacuated.

Now the only military action going on in the city was at the Green Line. On some nights, if we went to the top of our building, we could see the tracer rounds being shot back and forth between East and West Beirut and, every now and then, a stray shell would hit close to us or 50 caliber rounds would hit our building.

Since Beirut was now controlled by militias, we felt safe and started to venture down to the beach. I went to Ali's house overlooking the tennis courts to see if he could go swimming with me.

Before I could convince him to come to the beach, he said he wanted to show me something. He ran out into an open area across from his house and chased a chicken around for about ten minutes until he caught it.

I thought he wanted to kill it to eat it, but instead he said "Follow me" and started up the stairs. I ran behind him all the way to the fifth floor of the building and onto the roof.

I asked him, "What are you going to do with the chicken?"

He said he was going to throw it off from the top floor.

I said "Why don't you just shoot it instead of throwing it off the roof?"

He smiled and said, "Watch this."

He stretched his arms out and tossed the light brown chicken into the air. I was expecting the chicken to just fall straight down and splatter on the roadway, but instead, the chicken flapped its wings furiously fast and began descending in a circular pattern, missing the power lines, and landing in the open area by the tennis courts.

We had just found a new sport. We ran down, grabbed the chicken again, and watched him fly in circles three more times. The chicken did not seem to be agitated and showed no signs of stress or resistance. Although running up and down the stairs wore us out and we were too tired to continue, the chicken seemed ready to go again.

While we were resting and watching the chicken, a flatbed truck stopped at the trash pile up the street from Ali's house and dumped five or six big pieces of Styrofoam that looked like they came from a refrigerator. A couple of our other friends joined us as we pulled them out of the trash and decided to make a raft out of them. My friend Fadi was a mechanic's assistant. He showed us the best way to tie them together and we headed for the beach with our new raft. One of my friends picked up two sticks along the way to use as paddles. Once we crossed the boardwalk, people driving in cars were honking at us because they knew we had to be crazy to put a Styrofoam raft into the Mediterranean.

We stopped beside the Army base and put our clothes and shoes on the rocks. We got into the water and pushed off on the raft. It was a strong raft; it held all four of us. About a half a mile out to sea, we started to hear popping noises. We knew it wasn't the raft. A few minutes later the popping noise came closer and we looked around and all we could see was a white yacht.

We could see people on the deck with machine guns firing in our direction. As they got closer to us, we started to hear the bullets whizzing over our heads. I quickly gave one of my friends a paddle and told him to start paddling faster toward the shore. In a few minutes, the bullets started getting closer and closer, lower and lower over us, and then, suddenly, the army base started to return fire with a much heavier caliber machine gun. We were caught in the middle of a firefight!

When we started to see the tracer rounds go only a few feet over us, I dove off the raft and started swimming as if I were an Olympic gold medalist. My friends started calling me as they tried to paddle faster, but to no avail. They decided to abandon the raft and follow me. The gunfight was so intense and we were so scared that when I turned around my friends were already right behind me. I was amazed at their speed, but as kids we learned in the war that fear can make you run and, apparently, swim much faster.

We left all our stuff at the beach and ran toward home. When we got to the top of the hill, we stood behind a low concrete wall to see the gunfight between the yacht and the army base. Finally, the army base was able to correct its aim and black smoke came out of the yacht, indicating a direct hit.

The yacht slowly turned around and headed back toward East Beirut. So now we learned that we had to keep our eyes open for these yachts as well as gunboats. This kind of thing started to happen more frequently. The next morning we ran back down to the beach and found our belongings intact.

\* \* \*

Since West Beirut was now run by militias, you could get away with anything and another new sport was discovered: dynamiting fish. One of my uncles was a great contributor to this sport. Since most of the Eloud family liked fishing, this new method made it easier for them to bring the fish to the water's surface.

One morning, our houses shook from a funny sounding explosion we had not heard before. There was an explosion every hour, muffled explosions, but they still made our building shake. We discovered that dynamite was being used for fishing. Curious about this new sport, we went down to the beach to see it for ourselves. I wanted to know how it was done.

There was a marina there in an area that extended into the water next to a sewer that poured into the Mediterranean, a marina used by local fisherman near the base. Along the peninsula were upright barrels of concrete where fisherman could stand and cast into the sea. I watched two older men "fishing" there.

One stood on a barrel while the other tossed pieces of bread into the sea. After the first fisherman finished tossing a whole bag of bread crumbs into the water, the other fisherman stood on the barrel with dynamite in hand. From there, he had a bird's eye view down into the water. He had a rock tied to the dynamite and lit a waterproof fuse when he thought there were enough fish in the water below him. He lit the fuse and tossed the dynamite into the center of where the bread was being eaten by the fish.

First, there was a thud from the underwater explosion followed by a tower of water shooting up into the sky. Immediately the water turned white and, within a few seconds, stunned fish started appearing closer to the top. Both fishermen put their masks on and jumped into the water carrying two mesh bags to scoop in all the fish that had floated to the top.

Since everybody was doing it, I asked my dad why he didn't do the same thing. He said that he would not use dynamite to kill fish. There was a better and safer way. To prove that he was right, my dad asked Yousef, a kid my age who lived near my grandmother's house, to build us a fishing cage which we had seen him make before. He was very good at it. It was round and one of the biggest ones we had seen with a funnel shaped opening inside. It took two days for him to build it.

On our way to a private beach, Sporting Club Beach next to Long Beach, we picked up a green plant which my dad tied to the bottom of the cage with wire. He had a long rope tied onto the handle of the cage. When we got to the Sporting Club, we went to the back where we used to jump off the top of the stairs into the Mediterranean Sea. We went down the stairs and my dad asked my brother and me to put our masks on and jump into the water to make sure that the cage went into the water in the upright position.

After the cage was in a good position, we climbed out of the water with the rope and tied it to the ladder. One of the lifeguards, Abu Abed, who had worked there for over thirty years and was a friend of my dad's, told my dad that he would keep an eye on it. That was about 8:30 in the morning.

We came back at 12:00 noon and my dad untied the rope from the ladder and started to pull it up but needed some help. It took four of us, tugging on the rope behind him, to lift the cage. As it got closer to the surface, we could see in the clear Mediterranean water a dark swirl in the cage and when it finally surfaced, we saw that it was full of fish. It took two of us to grab the handles, hold onto the ladder, and drag the cage onto the platform.

People at the beach stopped near us to watch all the fish flopping around in the cage. The cage was full to the top with fish and almost all of the green plant had been eaten. It took several hours for us to clean them all. We could not wait to show our mother all the fish we had caught that day. But, since there was no electricity and no way to freeze the fish, we gave much of it away and only took home to her what we could eat that day.

\* \* \*

Although the militias had chased the Lebanese Army away, there was still sporadic shelling that sometimes came close to our house although sometimes it was only at the Green Line.

My dad decided that he did not, in his mind, want me to become lazy, so he woke me up at 5:00 one morning to go down to the boardwalk at the beach and jog.

It was very quiet. We started toward the beach past a few packs of wild dogs, being careful not to make any noise so they wouldn't chase us. It only took a few minutes to get down to the boardwalk. Once there, we noticed that there were a lot of other people either jogging or walking for exercise. As we walked on the boardwalk toward the Green Line, we saw small Volkswagen buses that had espresso machines in them serving folks at the beach. Some had candy and umbrellas and chairs for their customers. There was one every twenty feet.

We were surprised at the number of people who were out there that early in the morning. As we passed between the American University of

Beirut and the sea, we saw the huge antenna used by the American University close to the water's edge. As soon as we passed by the antenna, we heard small arms' fire from the Green Line and a few explosions in the distance. We didn't pay any attention to it because it was something we heard daily.

Then, to our surprise, we heard a fifty caliber machine gun firing in the distance and within a few seconds, bright, white phosphorus bullets came tumbling and whizzing within a few feet of us. They would hit the boardwalk and bounce in all directions.

We quickly turned and ran in the direction we had come from when we heard more gunfire in the distance from the same fifty caliber gun, more phosphorus bullets passing over and around us. Everyone who had been sitting in the beach chairs in front of the espresso vans took off running. A couple of the van owners hopped into their vans and took off without even having time to shut the vans sliding doors, Styrofoam cups flying out the doors as they left the scene.

We were running as fast as we could when I turned around and looked at my dad, his face ghostly pale since we almost got killed while jogging for our health.

"Is this what you call exercise?" I yelled.

I started to laugh at him and told him, "Why don't you go back and run again."

He was quiet and never said a word to me about exercise after that day. I was happy that I didn't have to get up at 5:00 in the morning any more since it was bad enough that we barely got any sleep at night from the random gunfire and the few shells that fell around us.

The next day I went down to the tennis courts and my friends all said that they had experienced the same thing, but usually in the afternoons. They described the same rounds of a fifty caliber and the white phosphorous glow of the bullets as they bounced through the air. A few kids had some of the bullets that they had found and we could tell for sure that it was a fifty caliber round since we all had seen or played with them before.

As we were looking at the bullets, we noticed a huge truck pulling into the soccer field. As it got closer, we could see the Mercedes emblem on its front. To our surprise, when it turned sideways, we noticed that it was carrying a rocket launcher on its flatbed followed by a smaller pickup truck with long rockets hanging out the back of it. Of course, we ran down towards it.

There were four armed men with long, bushy black beards that started to load up the rocket launcher with something that looked like large suppositories. We got about forty or fifty feet from the rocket launcher and watched them as they loaded one rocket at a time. We knew that they were going to fire them very shortly and we had front-row seats for the action.

They took turns loading the rockets and when they finished loading up, the small pickup truck that was with them drove away with two guys, a battery, and two cables. One of the men put one cable on the negative side of the battery and before he put a cable on the positive side, another guy, who was standing on a dirt pile with a pair of binoculars in one hand and a walkie-talkie in the other looking towards East Beirut, gave instructions to the first guy as to the proper elevation for the rocket launcher so that the target would be hit.

Once we saw that it would be very soon, we ran towards the lighthouse because from there we could get a better view. As soon as the firing started, we knew to run home because we had learned from the past that every time something is fired from one area, the other side would retaliate.

From the top of the hill we saw the guy with the battery touch the cable to the positive side and quickly release it making only one rocket take off. A huge flame shot from the back of the rocket launcher, causing a red clay dust cloud to form. With a loud whishing noise, the rocket left the tube and got into the clouds within a few seconds. Then we heard it land with a muffled noise on the East side of Beirut.

We all jumped up and down with excitement. Then, we noticed the guy with the binoculars standing on the dirt mound wave with approval because he had seen that the rocket landed where he intended. Once that signal was given, the man with the battery cables clamped the red cable to the positive side of the battery and this time he left it there making the rocket launcher rock back and release all its rockets in one fluid motion.

Within thirty seconds, all thirty of the rockets had left their tubes. The color and the sight of the rockets going into the clouds so quickly and the huge red cloud of dust kicked up by the rockets exhaust held us briefly spellbound.

After seeing that, all fifteen to twenty kids yelled out "Allahu Akbar" and took off running as fast as we could, kids peeling away in different directions towards their homes so that when we arrived at the homes on our street, we were only a handful.

Wess and I went quickly up the stairs to tell my mother and dad what we had just seen. We made sure we all stayed in one section of the house since at any time there would be retaliatory fire from East Beirut. Then I realized how it seemed that mainly civilians, not the militia, would become the casualties from the retaliatory fire since the truck that had fired from my neighborhood had left the scene.

Nothing happened that night, but about 4:00 in the morning, we heard about fifteen to twenty shells in the distance. Within a few seconds, they had landed on top of the buildings along our street. Luckily, they were not the heavy 155 mm shells that had been used in the past.

We could see antennas falling from the rooftops and landing in the streets, some of them with the wires still connected. We hid in the hallway by the elevator because a few more shells came in and shook our building and those surrounding us. A few minutes later, it was quiet and we figured it was over since we did not hear any more shells in the distance.

We went to the back of the balcony where we thought we had heard one land nearby. The apartment building across from the mosque, which was taller than our building and whose owner had pigeon cages on his roof, had been hit by a shell which damaged one of the water pipes causing it to spray down the building. But, mainly the damage was to rooftops and no shells hit the streets.

The next day I went to school and one of my teachers said "What are you doing here?" We could hear shells landing close by as we were near the Green Line. I told her it was more fun to be stuck at school than home.

Some of the shells started to land closer; that's when she turned around and told me to go home right then. I turned around and started to walk home, taking my normal shortcut up the long stairs.

As I was going up the stairs, I opened my backpack and began eating one of the sandwiches that my mom had made me. Once I got to the top of the steps, which numbered about two hundred, I stopped to rest for a moment since I was only two blocks away from my house.

Suddenly, I heard a growl coming from underneath a nearby car. A mangy Rottweiler and what looked like a German shepherd, both foaming at the mouth and baring their teeth, came running towards me with great speed. I threw my left-over sandwich at them and ran in the opposite direction while reaching for my 9 mm pistol in my waistband and looking over my shoulder.

I noticed that the German shepherd had stopped to eat the sandwich, but the Rottweiler was only a few feet away from me. Within a second of him getting near me, I had chambered my gun and turned towards him, firing two rounds.

One hit in front of the dog and the second one got him in the chest or the neck just as he started to lunge towards me. He yelped and hit the ground, blood oozing out of his wound, as the German shepherd ran off after getting another sandwich from my book bag.

I was shaking but happy that if it weren't for the gun, I would have been their lunch. When I holstered my gun back into my waistband, I noticed the guards at the back of the Saudi Arabian Embassy had their guns drawn and had seen the whole thing unfold. I waved to them that I was okay, turned around, and headed home.

I didn't say anything to my mother that night, but from then on, every time I got to the top of the stairs, I already had my hand on my gun so they would never catch me off guard. That was one more reason why everyone in Beirut needed a gun. If the war didn't kill you, the wild dogs would.

\* \* \*

For a few days after the shelling, school was closed. This happened on a regular basis; there would be shelling, then a break in school, then a return to school, then more shelling.

Heading back to school after this particular shelling, I was anxious to see my friends again since there were only nineteen students in the school. We were very close because of the war. Since our numbers were small, we only occupied the library on the top floor. The school had rented out the other sections to a Lebanese school. Most of us in the library had our own cubicles where we kept our book bags. There were no lockers so somebody's lunch always seemed to be missing.

One day, our librarian, June Tamim, who was from Britain, asked to speak to me in private and I yelled out from behind my cubicle, "It wasn't me!"

She laughed and said, "Don't worry. You're not in trouble."

She was always smiling and had a good outlook on life. Everyone was always happy to see her. She asked me, while looking over my shoulder to make sure no one was listening, if I could get her a gun because she was scared for her safety since four Americans had already been kidnapped.

The ones who were kidnapped were from the American University of Beirut across the street from our school. We all knew about it because it was all over the news and in Time Magazine.

I looked at her and smiled and said, "What makes you think I can get a gun?"

She looked at me and said, "I think everybody in Beirut has a gun."

I could tell from her face that she was serious and scared at the same time. Once I figured that out, I asked her if she wanted an AK-47 or an M-16.

She said, "No, no. I want a small gun to put in my purse, a lady's gun."

I told her it was harder to find a small gun because mainly big guns were all over the place.

The next day I got her a few pictures and she said they were all too big for her purse. She finally picked a 25 caliber which would still kill someone at close range. It took me a few days to get her one. With the help of a friend, we got her the gun and then she wanted us to show her how to use it.

We went to the upstairs section of the library which had an opening that looked down on the main library. We showed her how to chamber the gun and to use the safety on it.

She was pointing the loaded gun in all kinds of directions, including mine. I had to show her all over again and tell her to please not point the gun at me.

She was happy with it since it was chrome and had what looked like a pearl handle. She thanked me and paid us for the gun.

I never told anyone, not even my mother, about arming my teacher, but this incident would reappear in my life years later in an unexpected way.

**Sam (front row, left) with the few remaining students at ACS in 1985-1986 school year.**

# Chapter 29
## Black Sheets and Sandbags

School was out for the summer and I was on the way to the tennis court to do my usual ball-boy job to make some extra money. A friend's brother pulled up next to me on his motorcycle and asked me if I wanted to go shooting at the Green Line and of course I said yes. He had an AK-47 strapped on his back and I pulled up my shirt to show him my 9 mm and told him I needed something bigger than that.

He said, "Don't worry. Where we are going, they have everything" which made me even more excited.

We were zooming between cars and the closer we got to the Green Line, the more bullet and shell holes appeared. Some alleys we had to cross quickly because of signs that said "Beware of sniper."

There were big canvas sheets hanging from balcony to balcony to keep the snipers from seeing down the alley. He pointed at a place where last week a sniper got a kid on a motorcycle. You could still see the blood stain that was left on the sidewalk. He was explaining how dangerous snipers are and that he only had a few seconds to cross a small opening. He drove fast and to my surprise there were a lot of people living in those buildings that were riddled with bullet holes and had severe structural damage. I had never seen so many bullet holes so close together.

We parked the bike. As we approached, some gunmen looked as if they were leaving the Green Line. They waved at us and we waved back. Then they stopped since they recognized my friend's brother and told him which building he needed to shoot from since that was where the action was. Without thinking, I hurried with him to the building which was heavily sandbagged.

As I looked around before we entered the buildings, there were sandbags against every window and outside of every doorway. There was a black sheet covering the entrance of the building and he motioned me to put the sheet back after I entered.

My first question was "What's with the sheet?"

He said they didn't want any light coming into the building thus preventing the opposite side from seeing any shadows.

The building had a funny smell to it, a mildew smell, since there were pipes leaking slowly down the walls and green stains where algae was growing. The floor was covered with debris, glass, pieces of metal, and so many shell cases that when you walked you almost had to slide your feet through them so you wouldn't slip. I slipped on them several times and landed on my back.

We could hear gunfire from the building and we could also hear return gunfire like fists banging against the building that we were in. We got to the second floor where we saw a rat that someone had recently shot, covered with flies and giving off a foul odor. We started to see in the darkness the cases of ammunition and rocket-propelled grenades down the hallway towards the rooms we were going to shoot from.

There was a guy standing guard at the entrance to one of the rooms and he recognized my friend's brother. They spoke briefly and then he pointed at me. The guard nodded and handed me his AK-47. He asked me if I had used one before. I laughed at him and he laughed back. He pointed us towards one of the rooms in the building that was available to shoot from since the rest of the building was filled with other armed men shooting towards East Beirut. Sand fell down on us as the building was riddled with bullets and barely standing. My friend's brother pointed me to a small opening and told me to shoot out of it while he would shoot from another window which was sandbagged.

Before firing, I looked through the small opening to see where my shots would land.

What I saw, what I realized at that moment, traumatized me for the rest of my life. East Beirut, a big city that once was filled with gardens, cars, commerce, and celebrations, was now dark and abandoned, trees growing up through the middle of the streets. Fire had covered the buildings in black soot, shells had dug deep pockets in the terrain, and burnt car skeletons were strewn across the city.

I was shocked in a way that is hard to explain to see such a horrific scene, shocked even though I lived in the middle of the war and heard shelling almost daily. But, I had never seen it from this perspective, from atop a building with the city lying in ruins below me, completely destroyed, completely abandoned, the buildings occupied mainly by gunmen and soldiers where once many families lived and businesses operated. Out of the whole war, nothing made me realize how bad it was until I looked out that window. I realized that we were all killing each other for nothing.

After a few moments, my friend's brother came over and asked, "What are you waiting for?"

I looked at him, returning from my thoughts, and asked him "Which building should I be shooting at?"

He pointed out a building that was slightly to our right and said that the Lebanese Army occupied that building. So, as if on autopilot myself, I pointed my gun in that direction and fired, my gun on full automatic making me jerk back and almost lose control. When that magazine was empty, I put a new one in and switched the gun to semi-automatic. I aimed at their sandbags and shot until I could see where my bullets were hitting.

As I was still shooting, one of the other guys from our building stepped out into the street with an RPG and fired his rocket toward the army building, hitting the same sandbags that I had targeted. I was startled because I didn't see him firing until it was over. Then he ran back into the building.

A few minutes later, while I was still shooting, we started receiving mortar fire. Two of them hit in front of the building causing more sand to fall on us and made everyone step away from the windows. More mortar rounds hit. We could not leave the building for two hours because they had us pinned down.

I noticed that my shoulder was bruised from the shooting I had done. I had never shot that many rounds before. The gun was still hot and ticking as I laid it up against the wall with the rest of the guns. It was time for me to go.

I didn't want my mother to find out why I was gone so long. After it got calm, we hopped on the motorcycle and headed home. We arrived at my house within ten minutes and I told Wess what I had done and of course, he thought that was really cool.

The whole night I couldn't sleep because all I could remember was the picture of the city in my head and how sad and abandoned it was. Shortly after that, I started to feel depressed.

One day, one of my cousins told me that if I brought my own bullets, we could go down to the Green Line across from the Phalangist building with its flag draped across its front. I quickly said yes and he said that he had a friend that lived a block from the Green Line who knew a member of Hezbollah that would let us use his gun as long as we brought our own bullets.

At home, I pulled out the drawer of our hiding place and took the bullets, including Wess's, and my cousin and I took a cab close to the Green Line to an area called Basta.

The cab dropped us off next to a mosque decorated with black flags. My cousin's friend lived across the street from the mosque and we walked up the stairs to meet him.

From there, we crossed the alley quickly to avoid sniper fire. The designated building was only a block away. We walked between buildings and climbed over a short wall where we found our friend with the AK-47. He was a bearded man in his early thirties and when I got close enough to shake his hand, I noticed a small white baby spider crawling in his beard. I didn't say anything for fear of offending him.

Our excitement heightened as we saw a building with the Phalangist flag flying from the second floor balcony only a few hundred feet away from us. We couldn't imagine how that building was still standing since it was riddled with bullets, large chunks of concrete blown out and rebar exposed. All the support beams were exposed, too, and were straining to keep the building upright. It reminded me of malnourished Ethiopian children, starved to the point of death, their bones exposed, pushing out against the skin.

We walked into the small three-story building. We could only use the ground level because the top floors had been hit so many times that it wasn't safe. My cousin and I closed the black sheet behind us and took turns shooting at a building across the street. We could also see an old church in the distance. A few blocks from the church was a mosque. And here as before, the crumbling concrete showered us from above as we fired. We were fortunate to be using AK-47s because any other less sophisticated weapons would have jammed from the falling debris. We only used single rounds to stretch out our time there as we only had so many bullets to use.

After firing two magazines, we decided to go to another location right around the corner from that building. There we had a good view of the Phalangist building with its flag across it.

I accidentally switched the gun to full automatic when it was my turn to shoot. Luckily, the Hezbollah member was standing behind me when I squeezed the trigger and fifteen rounds shot from the gun pushing me back and making some of the rounds go up in the air. He grabbed me by the waist preventing me from falling into a small stairwell nearby that had an iron gate.

After that, we ran from one end of the street to reach another building, also riddled with bullets but closer to the Phalangist building. After my friend began the run to the other building, a sniper round was fired in my direction and hit just a few feet over my head. We all ducked down, happy that someone was shooting back.

After my cousin ran to the building, it was my turn to go. I started to run but tripped over some tin cans and other debris. As they yelled at me to run faster, I got up and started to run again but slipped on some shell casings and fell one more time. I thought I was still safe because of the dirt mounds piled in the street. They had been there so long that grass and small shrubs were growing on them.

As I got up, another round passed over my head but this time I just walked because when I tried to run, I kept falling. They yelled at me to run faster, but I ignored them and kept walking until I got to the building.

My cousin looked at me and said, "What, are you crazy?"

"What kind of sniper was that," I said, brushing myself off, "who couldn't shoot me after falling three times?"

We took more turns shooting from that position since many more buildings across the street were exposed to us. After we ran out of bullets, we received more return fire because they had figured out where we were. We decided to run back to where we had been when we heard small-arms fire hit the sandbags in front of the building.

# Chapter 30
## Rambo Comes to Beirut

We thanked the guy for letting us use his gun. He smiled and said, "Next time you have some more bullets, come down. I will be glad to take you out again." Although our adrenalin was pumping, we couldn't tell our other friends for fear that my mother might find out.

The next day we found out that the movie "Rambo" was playing in a theatre not far from my house or the Green Line. A group of us decided to go.

Even though there was no electricity, the theater had a generator. This theater was at the end of Al Hamra Street. Max, our neighborhood dog, followed us all the way to the theater, barking at anyone who got close to us.

To our surprise, when we got to the theater, there were about fifty militia men carrying their guns, their jeeps all parked outside the theater. They were all going to see the same movie we were. Of course, we were admiring all their guns as they walked in with us. Some of them didn't even pay and the usher taking the tickets at the door didn't dare say a word to them.

There was a big banner showing Rambo, Sylvester Stallone, spread across the front of the theater. He was wielding a 30 caliber machine gun with a belt of bullets draped over one arm. He was bare-chested with a red cloth rag tied around his head, his arm muscles bulging as he fired his weapon.

The theater was packed. Everybody was talking loudly until the movie started. For us, it was a motivational movie. We grew up in the war and thought of ourselves and each other as the many Rambos of Beirut.

When the scene came on where Rambo rescued the POWs and was trying to fly back to an American base in a Huey helicopter, a huge Soviet armed helicopter following him, the crowd was on the edge of their seats.

Then, Rambo's helicopter was hit and smoke began pouring from it. Rambo landed the helicopter into the shallow part of the river and he appeared to pass out. When the Soviet helicopter approached him, facing him head on, the Russian commander was smiling because he had the Huey in his sights and was ready to blow up Rambo and the helicopter.

Suddenly, out of the audience in front of us, an armed gunman stood up, yelled "Allahu Akbar" and emptied an entire AK-47 magazine into the Russian helicopter on the screen. Everybody ducked down, but some people were hit with flying shell cases.

Then, on the screen, Rambo got up and fired a hand-held Law missile through his helicopter windshield, the rocket hitting the Russian helicopter and destroying it. In fear and excitement, everyone in the theater jumped up and yelled "Allahu Akbar," and a few people fired their pistols into the air. You could hear chunks of concrete falling from the ceiling.

We were terrified from the incident, but relieved at the same time that Rambo got the bad guy.

Shortly after that scene, the movie was over. Everyone walking out of the theater was pumped up after seeing the best war-action movie of the eighties. All the gunmen in the theater talked about going down to the Green Line since they just watched Rambo and each one of them thought he was Rambo.

Max was standing outside the theater wagging his tail when he saw us and started to follow us back home. Within a few minutes of getting home, the Green Line had erupted and we knew what caused it. Rambo had influenced not just us kids, but also the militias. We heard that a popular guy on the Phalangist side in East Beirut who looked like Rambo was later interviewed for a documentary about the war.

# Chapter 31
## The Armenian Bottle Lady

As we started to go back to school, militias in West Beirut began fighting against each other. The first militia that was eliminated was the popular Sunni militia, the Murabitoon. During this war-within-a-war, most of the Murabitoon fighters were either killed or joined other militias. Sometimes there would be intense fighting in small neighborhoods causing a lot of collateral damage giving us kids some new scenes of devastation to visit. It was as if we were getting ready for the Super Bowl and teams were being eliminated until there were only two.

The days that school was closed, I would go to the lighthouse and help a relative of mine, the mechanic mentioned earlier. If work was slow there, my friends and I would spray paint the walls with our gang name, "Zombies." We got into rock fights and threw glass Pepsi bottles at other kids who wandered into our neighborhood with bad intentions. The gang grew quickly and there was even another branch at my school, ACS. We even wrote the gang name on our Lebanese currency and a year later, one of our friends called to tell us that the change he had gotten back from a store had our Zombie logo on it.

One morning, an old Armenian lady who constantly talked to herself in her native language and lived in the bottom of the partly demolished building next to the Saudi Arabian Embassy, came down our street with a rusty shopping cart she used to collect glass bottles. When some kids from another neighborhood approached her and started to harass her, we knew something was wrong because she started to yell, making the kids in our gang grab rocks and bottles and head her way.

As soon as we got within range, we unleashed a barrage of rocks and Pepsi bottles towards the kids who were harassing her. They did not realize we were that close until they turned around and were being pelted by incoming rocks and bottles. They tried to grab rocks to throw back at us, but there were so many of us throwing rocks and bottles that they hardly had a chance to throw anything at us. They ran as fast as they could, one of them holding his hand on his head after being struck by a rock, blood running down his face. We chased them all the way down the street until we couldn't see them anymore with Max behind us barking in their direction and continuing to chase them while we retreated.

When the lady saw me coming back, she handed me a glass bottle to thank me, but I didn't know what to do with the bottle. As soon as she turned around to collect more bottles from the trash, I quietly put it back into her shopping cart and walked away.

* * *

More fighting erupted in West Beirut between different militias weekly. Sometimes it would be safe to go on the beach when fighting was taking place in other areas of West Beirut.

One morning I went down to the tennis courts where the American Embassy had relocated after it was bombed. One of my cousins was in charge of the security detail at the embassy. As I got on the stairs going down to the tennis courts, Pony, the tennis court dog that everyone in the area including me fed, came to greet me as I began to whistle for him. As I petted him, I looked out to the Mediterranean Sea and noticed another yacht that was coming from the East Beirut side and getting closer. I asked my friends at the tennis courts if they noticed that the boat seemed to be getting a little closer and they said yes.

We waved at one of the guards positioned on top of the American Embassy where a fifty-caliber machine gun was mounted behind a short semi-circular wall. The wall had bullet-proof windows that could be opened or closed by a rope pull. We waved at the guard while pointing toward the boat. He took out his binoculars and looked where we pointed.

About fifteen minutes later, the boat had gotten much closer and now we could see more of its detail. The boat fired in our direction. We kept yelling at the embassy guard and he said that he couldn't fire back until the bullets flew over the embassy. So, we all stood behind one of the tennis court walls to shield ourselves from bullets flying over the tennis courts.

Within a few seconds, the embassy guard swiveled his machine gun in the direction of the boat and opened fire. He hit close to the boat, white splashes rising where the bullets landed.

Within minutes, two pickup trucks pulled up in the soccer field adjacent to the tennis courts and facing the sea. With single anti-aircraft barrels mounted on each one, they took up positions at the far edge of the soccer field, protecting themselves behind a small dirt mound. We wanted a better view, so we ran up the hill with my friends Ahmed and Mohammed, instructors at the tennis courts. It was the perfect location to see both the anti-aircraft guns and the boat all at once.

When the anti-aircraft guns started to fire, it was much louder than the fifty-caliber atop the embassy. You could see the anti-aircraft rounds exploding both in front of and behind the boat. The gunners then readjusted their aim, trying to center it more. Then, one of the anti-aircraft guns malfunctioned and stopped firing and we could see the militia men trying to fix the problem.

The other anti-aircraft gunner decided to start shooting from the shore line into the water, slowly walking the bullets all the way to the boat. After a second try, the gunner was successful. You could see the anti-aircraft rounds exploding right at the water line in front of the boat's hull. With a direct hit, black smoke began rolling out of the boat.

Finally, the fifty-caliber machine gun rounds from the embassy began to hit the target also. Heavy smoke continued to roll out of the boat as it started to pull away, heading toward East Beirut. Everyone at the tennis courts started to cheer. My friends and I began to yell, you guessed it, "Allahu Akbar."

The shooting continued in the boat's direction, but now the boat was getting out of range. As we were still watching all this unfold, one of my cousins from the Druze militia arrived in an armored personnel carrier with a fifty-caliber machine gun mounted on top, ready to join in the fight. But, when he arrived, the boat was out of range. So, instead, he started to do doughnuts with the armored personnel carrier in the center of the soccer field, causing a huge red dust cloud to rise up into the sky. After the boat had limped away and all the guns were quiet, it was business as usual back at the tennis courts for a while.

A more intense level of fear was caused by car bombings. There were two to three car bombings a week in both sides of the city, East and West. It would happen at the busiest time of day near churches, mosques, markets, and schools. The car bombs caused such intense devastation that it rocked the city and caused horrific damage for blocks on end.

Some of the car bombs were so powerful that bodies were found many blocks away from the explosions. We became so alert to any possibility of a car bomb that we kept an eye on all cars as well as who drove into our neighborhoods.

In one incident, an old Mercedes was double-parked next to Corner Sport and everyone on the street yelled asking whose car that was. We all ran to our balconies to signal to all that the car did not belong to us. After twenty minutes of yelling and honking, a man with a mustache showed up to claim his car.

He was yelled at, shoved around the street, and almost beaten until one person intervened, got him into his car, the car surrounded by a mob of angry neighbors. From our balcony, Wess and I cussed at him and called him all kinds of names for scaring the hell out of all of us.

Two days later, a car loaded with explosives was found in front of the mosque that was behind our building. Luckily, someone saw some wires coming from beneath the hood of the car which raised suspicion. Soon after that, the car bomb was diffused, making us feel fortunate but tense as it was so close to home. We became paranoid and streets were barricaded with big square concrete blocks so no cars could enter.

Some militia men took advantage of the car bombing situation and started asking store owners for money, protection money. If the storeowner refused to pay, a stick of dynamite or a grenade was tossed at the stores during the night. Other stores got the message quickly and started paying militia members money so nothing would happen to their stores. Here's an example.

One night about 8:00, Wess and I were at the back balcony of our home facing the mosque. The full moon, not electricity, illuminated all the buildings and the streets below. With our binoculars, we were looking at the details in the full moon. As the city was dark, it was easier to see the moon's detail. Within a few minutes of looking through the binoculars, we saw a huge explosion with red shrapnel and metal flying through the air. It looked as if it were only two blocks away.

We ducked behind the concrete balcony wall and seconds later we heard the explosion. We weren't scared since we had already seen the blast before we heard it. We knew it was close by, but we did not know what the target was. My mother turned on the radio and after a few minutes the newscaster reported where it had landed. To our shock, it was Smith's Supermarket, where my mother frequently shopped. Minutes later, we could smell the burning of the store.

The next morning, my friends and I arrived at the scene to see the carnage. There was glass in the street, broken bottles, and workers moving the charred refrigeration cases outside. Cans of food expanded from the heat were ready to explode. All the soda cans had exploded and people were still rummaging through the store trying to see if anything was salvageable.

We looked for batteries and candles since they were essential in a war zone, but they were all burned beyond recognition. We could see the soot caused by the fire extending up the walls of the building. We heard that one of the workers, who happened to be in the building, died from smoke inhalation when he ran upstairs and could not open the door of the roof to escape the smoke. Workers found him dead at the roof door.

There was increased street fighting between militias in West Beirut. There was a gun battle in our street one night where a rocket-propelled grenade was accidentally launched by my cousin when he tripped over the tram tracks in front of the Saudi Arabian Embassy.

The grenade hit the second floor of our building causing a small hole in the concrete balcony and shattering the glass sliding doors on the first and second floors. Since these rounds are made to be used against metal tanks or armored vehicles instead of concrete, the damage was minimal, but the sound was very loud. If it had hit a tank or other metal object, the hot copper in the grenade would have penetrated the thick metal skin of the tank with a molten jet of copper, disabling the vehicle and probably killing its occupants.

The next morning, everything was quiet and everyone was in the streets pointing at where the grenade had hit. You could hear the scraping of dustpans scooping up the glass as residents cleaned their balconies of debris. If it had hit a few inches higher, it would have hit the living room of the second floor occupants who were playing cards in the candlelight.

Later, when I saw my cousin, who was a lot older, I asked him jokingly why he didn't aim it a little higher and blow us out of our apartment. He laughed and told me it was an accident and how he had tripped over the tram tracks.

The next night, a huge gun battle took place between our street and the street where the mosque was located. My friend Omar's brother, Ahmed, who belonged to the Sunni militia, had a heavy machine gun that made a distinctive noise when fired. It could be recognized easily over any other shots being fired.

We were in bed that night and stayed still in our beds while the gunfight took place all around us. Our bedroom wall was hit with a few rounds, but because it was thick concrete, the rounds did not penetrate. The gunfight intensified in our street and we could hear cars being hit by bullets and ricocheting between metal balcony posts. After a few hours, the distinctive noise of Ahmed's gun had stopped, making us wonder what was going on.

Twenty minutes later, we heard the siren of the Volkswagen bus used by that militia to carry its wounded or its fighters, who were all able to cram inside the bus, it seats having been removed. They hung with their guns outside the windows of the bus. It arrived in our street and six people jumped out with their guns drawn and ran to Omar's house at about 5:00 in the morning.

Then we heard a piercing scream from Omar's mother making everyone in the neighborhood look out their balconies as it was almost daylight and the gunfire had dwindled.

When morning came, we were told that Ahmed, Omar's brother, had received a gunshot wound in the back of his head and was at American University Hospital in critical condition. It would take two weeks for Ahmed to recover enough to come home. Even then, the back of his head was covered with bandages.

We walked outside and down the street that morning to survey the damage. We saw all the cars on our street had bullet holes in them, including our Volkswagen bug. Its windows were shattered and you could see where the bullet had entered and, like investigators, we checked the entry and exit points of the bullets. We counted at least eight rounds that had passed through the car and its seats. Wess and I hoped all this damage would convince our dad to get a new car. We had had that car for many years and my dad was so cheap that he did not even put a radio in it. But, to our disappointment, the engine was in perfect condition, located as it was in the back of the car.

Not too long after that, there was an explosion near the mosque. The Volkswagen bus used by the militia was parked in front of its headquarters, a few doors down from the mosque. The story was that someone drove by and tossed an explosive device into the bus, not killing anyone but destroying the bus.

The fighting between militias started to get out of control and the Syrian army came back into the city to stop the fighting. They had roadblocks on every major corner and would stop and search cars randomly and still they would walk to the back of a VW bug and ask you to open the trunk.

At these checkpoints, they would take anything they wanted out of the car, including my Michael Jackson cassette tapes. Nobody would dare say anything to them. But, their presence did help the city to quiet down except for areas around the Green Line.

Summer was coming to an end and schools were ready to reopen, but now the Syrians, with their artillery guns, started bombarding East

Beirut daily. In return, the Phalangists, with great accuracy, started to return fire on the Syrian positions inflicting heavy damages to the Syrian forces. Some shells even landed right in the sandbagged openings from which the Syrians were shooting.

# Chapter 32
## Saying Goodbye

I had had enough. I told my school friends and teachers that I was not going to come back to school that year. Everyone looked surprised. I had gotten to the point where I didn't care whether I went to school or got shot. Nothing seemed worth the effort anymore. Why bother with school or anything else when I had seen the future from that window at the Green Line and it was bleak.

Around this time, a cousin of mine and his wife were visiting from the U.S. My dad, concerned about my safety and declining mood, approached him and asked if I could go to the states and live with them since the situation had escalated in Beirut. Soon the airport would be shutting down and there would be no way to leave. He asked me not to tell my mother because we knew she would freak out if I was going to leave.

He got me flight tickets and two days before departure, I told my mom, who was visibly upset and shocked. None of us knew our cousin that well as he had been living in the U.S. for many years. I was excited to be leaving, to see something new, and was looking forward to living somewhere that had continuous electricity, running water, and a phone that actually had a dial tone as soon as you picked it up.

I decided to give the grenade I had hidden to a friend of mine at school and I told him to keep the rubber band wrapped around the spoon/safety just in case the pin was pulled. I told him that if anything happened to him, I was not responsible. We both laughed because if anything happened, he would not be around to blame me anyway.

I gave my 9 mm handgun to another friend at school who drove a yellow Mercedes. He pulled out the dashboard radio, slid the gun into the opening, and then reinserted the radio back in its position. It was like something out of James Bond.

After that I felt naked, since I did not have my pistol tucked in my waistband or access to my grenade.

I went down to the tennis courts, hugged and kissed all my friends, stopped by the mechanic's shop underneath the lighthouse and gave them all hugs and kisses. I saluted the members of my gang, the Zombies, including the ones at my school.

I said goodbye to Zina, my Palestinian girlfriend, who was upset with me for leaving.

In my neighborhood, I said goodbye to Omar and his family, the Armenian pharmacist whose shop was on the ground floor of our building, and the mayor who owned the coffee shop across the street.

I said my goodbyes to the owner of Corner Sport and Ahmed, the parrot, who was still busy whistling and cussing as women walked by.

I said my goodbyes to the tenants in our building, the concierge and his family, and my cousins who lived near my grandmother, and I petted Max for the last time. Later on, he disappeared and no one knew what happened to him.

And of course, when I said my goodbyes to Wess, I told him not to forget to water the Syrian owner's plants on his way up to the roof.

My mother was very distraught that I was leaving. And I felt sick about having to leave her and my brothers in that turmoil. But, I was also excited about starting a new life and hoped they could be part of it soon.

Part II
1986-1994

# Chapter 33
## From Beirut to Richmond

In September of 1986, my cousin and his new wife met us at the airport where we boarded a British Airways plane and headed out to England. From England, we flew to Dulles International Airport in Washington, D.C.

On the way there, I was excited and sad at the same time because I was leaving all my family, all my friends, and everything I knew behind. My cousin talked with me a few times during the flight about the things that I liked, asking me specifically what kind of music I liked. He used to be a D.J. when he was younger and had a lot of stereo equipment in the U.S.

Once we arrived at Dulles, we were picked up by his brother-in-law and driven to Richmond, Virginia. I was amazed by how long it took us to get there because in Lebanon, the airport was only five minutes away. I was shocked to see such big highways and no trash on the streets. And, people actually stopped at red lights whereas in Lebanon they were used for target practice. Everything looked clean and there was no evidence of war or potholes as big as cars and all the lanes were marked properly.

Once we got into Richmond, we drove to Glen Allen, a suburb west of the city. Compared to the city life in Beirut with its tall residential buildings, the single-family homes in Glen Allen rose no more than two stories and there was not one bullet hole in any of them, no one walking around with any guns, and not an armored personnel carrier or tank in sight.

We got to my cousin's house and pulled into his gravel driveway. Their cat, Frisky, came out to greet us. It was starting to get dark, so I could not see that much of the neighborhood.

I had a hard time sleeping that night because it was so quiet. In the morning, I saw a squirrel outside my window, the first time I had ever seen a squirrel. I almost went looking for my gun and then remembered that we were in the U.S. and you couldn't do things like that over here.

I was amazed at how many trees there were around us everywhere, because in Lebanon, when I looked out of my bedroom window, I could see the Mediterranean, and from the back balcony, I could see mountaintops in the distance, no trees blocking the views.

I was already two weeks late for school, so we had to rush to a doctor's office to get immunizations before registering at Hermitage High School. I also had to take an English entrance exam, on which I did surprisingly well, and began my senior year.

I was surprised at how clean and nice the public school looked. Everything looked brand new. I was also impressed by the number of kids who went to school because in Lebanon, there were only eighteen to twenty kids in school during the war. In this sprawling school, I almost needed a map to find my way to class. The teachers were nice and wanted to help me out, especially in my U. S. History and Government classes, that being so new to me.

In World History class, I seemed to know more about the Middle East and everybody would ask me if Lebanon was a desert with camels running around. I would smile and say that Lebanon has no deserts, and if we did have camels, they would have two humps making them a luxurious stretch limousine. Very few people knew about the war in Lebanon even though it was on the news ninety percent of the time. Whenever our government teacher gave us an assignment, I would bring in current articles on the war in Beirut.

After a few months in school, I became accustomed to the American lifestyle, but I was still shocked that all the government buildings had no guards and no sandbags around them for protection. The police, or cops as the kids called them, only carried small pistols, while in Lebanon they carried AK-47s with multiple magazines. Whenever we drove by a government building or a police station, in my mind I would see where the sandbags needed to go, where the fifty-caliber could be mounted on top of the buildings, and where roadblocks could be set up to avoid suicide car bombers.

I still did not sleep well, feeling uneasy from the quietness of the night since I was accustomed to hearing guns firing in the background or a random explosion from a stray shell.

Another surprise to me was was how much makeup the girls in high school began to wear at such a young age. I liked the girls so much that I enrolled in a Home Economics cooking class when I discovered that it was all girls and I would be the only boy in the class. I felt like a prince surrounded by a harem because most of them did my cooking homework assignments for me. When some of them questioned why I couldn't do it, I told them that we had metric measurements for cooking in Lebanon and I didn't know how to convert them to the U.S. measurements.

My cousin suggested that I should start working because, as an additional member of the household, I caused their expenses to increase. He asked me to call my dad and ask him to send him money for me on a monthly basis. Neither my father nor my cousin told me the amount he sent. Later, I found that it was a $1,000 a month, a lot of money at the time.

At my cousin's request, I took a job at a Safeway grocery store as a bag boy, working after school from 4:30 to closing at 11:00. I mopped all the aisles at night and took out the trash. I didn't mind the work, but I didn't have time to eat anything after school and before work. No snack, no dinner, nothing.

One day I took a loaf of bread from the bakery department, took it to the employee break room, and ate almost the whole loaf of bread with a half a bottle of ketchup that was always on the break room table. I had to eat it quickly so nobody would see me. Later, when I realized that my cousin was getting $1,000 a month from my dad to help pay for my stay, I was angry that I had stooped to stealing a loaf of bread when there should have been money for me to buy a snack or dinner to eat in the break room. I never saw any of the money my dad sent and to top it off, I had to hand over all my paychecks to my cousin.

For the first time in my life, I saw snow falling. That snow shut down the schools and since my cousin was out of town traveling, his wife went to stay with her parents. Before leaving, my cousin turned down the thermostat in the house to 60 degrees and told me to leave it there. We had about a foot of snow that year and I had to wear my coat inside the house to stay warm.

Kevin, whom I met at Hermitage, became a good friend, his dad and grandparents being of Lebanese descent. He came over during the snowstorm for a visit since he lived in the same neighborhood. When he got into the house, he commented that it was warmer outside than it was in the house. So we decided to go over to his house to warm up.

I got to meet his mom and dad, his sister Tonya, and his little brother Mark. They greeted me as if I were family and our friendship grew as the weeks went by.

Kevin and his friends took me to the high school football games with them even though I didn't know anything about football except the part of hitting each other, which was the best part of the game. I made a lot of friends at school. Most had cars, which I didn't, and they would give me rides home from school instead of having to ride the big yellow bus, which everyone in high school hated to ride.

I was very homesick and would spend a lot of nights writing letters to my friends in Lebanon. I would still see the news and see areas in Beirut near my house being shelled. It made me very anxious about my parents and my brothers. Calling them was always difficult because the phone lines in Beirut were often down.

After quitting my job at Safeway, I found a job at Westower Cinemas, which was more fun and less labor intensive. Plus, I got to see all the movies that came out. It also had a nice arcade area which reminded me of Beirut, where one of the only things available to kids during the war was arcades in buildings that had their own generators.

My cousin kept insisting that I join the U.S. military since I was an American citizen. He really just wanted to get me out of his house. He took me to a U. S. Armed Forces Recruiting Station on West Broad Street in the Tuckernuck Shopping Center. And again I was surprised that there would be a military recruiting station in a shopping center with no security in sight, not even security cameras. An even bigger surprise was that none of the recruiters were armed. That would never happen in the Middle East.

My cousin suggested that I join the Air Force since my dad was an airline pilot. Later on, at a different recruiting station, I took an Air Force test, quickly jotting down any answers because I had no intention of joining. I had already seen enough war to last me a lifetime. The young recruiters, on the other hand, had little or no firsthand knowledge of war duty as this was 1987 and the U.S. military had not seen real war since Vietnam.

Other times, I was called to come back to the recruiting station to see if I was interested in other branches of the military. I told them that I hadn't decided yet and they said they would continue to follow up with me.

As I left the recruiting station, I thought to myself that a place like this in Beirut would not last five minutes. Anyone could walk in and out as they pleased without a security guard or a metal detector to stop them. The station reminded me of the Marine barracks in Beirut which had been so vulnerable to attack.

After I graduated from Hermitage High School, my cousin got me a five gallon bucket of paint and asked me to paint the outside of the house. I had never painted anything in my life, but had seen it done before. He got me a ladder and I spent a month on that ladder, except for the few times I fell off. Luckily, I landed in the grass and, more importantly, no one saw me fall.

Every time Kevin and my friends would come over, they would pull up in their cars and ask me to come with them. Of course I couldn't because I had to finish painting the house and then cut the grass. After a while, when Kevin told his dad about what was going on with me, they asked me if I wanted to move in with them. I gladly did and my cousin was also happy that he didn't have that responsibility anymore.

I was excited to move in with the Fahed family because they treated me like one of their own kids, not like a slave. They took me with them on vacation to Emerald Isle, South Carolina, the first time since being in the states that I had seen clear ocean water.

While talking with some of the guys I worked with at the movie theater, I found out that they were into collecting guns and ammo. One of them was interested in selling his AK-47, but I didn't respond to him because at the time I saw no need for it.

Shortly after that, I started working with Kevin's dad, Mr. Fahed, fixing water pumps and generators at a building down the street from the Hanover airport. It was the most adventurous job I had had because we went to different locations every day, even went to the sewage treatment plant in Richmond where they had huge open tanks for processing sewage.

There was a huge pump in the middle of each tank which sprayed sewage into the air, killing the bacteria. When we removed one of those pumps to take back to the shop, my job was to hose it down with a power washer before it was taken apart and worked on. I learned quickly to wear goggles and keep my mouth shut while I power-washed the dirt and sewage off the pump. Once the pump was repaired, my job was to spray paint it and clean its electrical cord.

Every week we were working at a different location which is how I got to know the James River which runs through Richmond. Mr. Fahed, his assistant, and I went down to the James to work on a barge, something I had never seen before. The barge was used to carry heavy construction equipment from one side of the river to the other. Water pumps were used on the barge to either fill the barge with water or pump water out to make the barge level with the ramps on the shore so the equipment could be loaded or unloaded

Every time I looked at the river, I could see Phalangist gunboats sneaking up on us and opening fire. But then I would remind myself that I was in the U.S. and that there were no gunboats on the James River.

Later on that year, work slowed for Mr. Fahed and he decided to build a house on Pouncey Tract Road in Henrico County outside of Richmond. On days that we were slow at the shop, we would drive to the house that was being built and do all the electrical wiring. While he installed electrical outlets, I drilled holes in the wall studs for the wires to pass through. It was interesting to see how a house was built from the ground up.

Later on, I found out that across from Innsbrook Office Park, a pizza place was opening soon and when Mr. Fahed told me that the owner was Lebanese, I decided to go there and apply for a job. I was the first one to be hired and was there for the grand opening. Since there were no other pizza places in the area at the time, we were very busy and worked picked up quickly.

After Mr. Fahed completed the house, we moved in and were enjoying suburban life, a deer or two wandering through the yard every now and then.

Mr. Fahed had two dogs that would go crazy when I got home because I always smelled of pizza. I learned how to make the pizzas, even tossing them in the air and catching them which didn't take long to master since I practiced all day.

I started seeing more things on the news about Lebanon and I was completely engrossed in the escalating situation between East and West Beirut. I would see footage of Syrian forces down the street from my house while heavy shelling resumed between the East and West. Even while I was at work, I would think about it and worry about my family and friends.

While I was working at Leonardo's, I purchased a small 22 caliber pistol from a friend with the intention of shooting squirrels and for protection when I went to shoot pool at The Playing Fields in Richmond, an area where I did not feel as safe as I did in the suburbs where I lived. I told no one about my gun purchase.

The war in Lebanon kept escalating and more footage of the fighting was shown on TV. I was getting very frustrated at how bad life was in Beirut and how people in other parts of the world, including the U.S., had no clue as to what was really going on. It was as if everyone was sitting safely in an arena watching while the fighting and the killing and the occupying of Lebanon was taking place. I kept thinking of how my parents and brothers were doing and if there was a way to get them out. I learned that getting my family out of Beirut would take a lot of money and a lot of red tape, which made me even more frustrated.

I kept reliving the war in my mind and the many close calls we had had with death. Here I was in the U.S. where there was no danger to me from militias fighting one another and I had left all my friends and family behind in the worst of circumstances. I also thought of the orphanages that we visited in Lebanon as kids and seeing all those children horribly maimed by explosives during the war. Most of the unexploded Israeli bombs that we would find had serial numbers and were stamped "Made in the U.S.A." When I thought about that at the time, it made me even angrier since all the taxpayers in the United States did not know that a lot of their money was being spent on supplying Israel and the Lebanese Phalangists with shells and ammunition that kept the Lebanese civil war going for many years. Even after the civil war, more militias were supplied with an abundance of American-made arms and ammunition.

Sleep became ever more difficult because every night there would be news showing Syrian troops shelling East Beirut with great intensity. I knew that the Syrians had assumed their old positions on the soccer field close to our home in Beirut, but this time, they used the field as an artillery base surrounded by barrels full of rocks and sand, barriers set up for their protection. But still, Phalangist accuracy was deadly, and sometimes they would take out the Syrian artillery positions.

I felt somebody needed to do something to stop the insanity since Lebanon was always on the news and nobody was doing anything about it. Whenever I heard aid was given to Lebanon, I knew that the supplies given were really ammunition to keep the war going.

Having grown up in the war, I knew that all the politicians there were looking out for themselves while the country was being devastated. I had seen many people wandering the streets of Beirut talking to themselves, homeless people digging through trash, people in wheelchairs from having stepped on landmines, people suffering severe and debilitating depression and other mental illnesses caused by war. Even animals were running abandoned in the streets, some missing legs or eyes or bearing other horrible deformities. I asked myself why the Lebanese people should endure all that pain and suffering while the rest of the world has moved on in life while the lives of the Lebanese seemed to be stuck on pause.

Everyone talked about Lebanon, but no one would do anything about it. I felt I owed my country, my friends, and my family. Those who left for safe haven never went back to help those left behind. I did not want to be one of them.

I knew something had to be done and soon. What other place would be better to get attention than the local U.S. Armed Forces Recruiting Station, the one I had often visited?

Unlike the armies in Lebanon, the U.S. military in recent years had not dealt with militant factions at home, their wars being fought mostly on foreign soil. No one would ever expect a recruiting station to be confronted in such a manner in broad daylight. I needed to plan carefully but it would be the best way, I thought, to bring media attention to the plight of Lebanon, especially in Richmond where nothing of that caliber had ever taken place.

**Sam at Empire State Building while visiting family
in New York, 1986.**

**Sam during the 1986 visit to New York**

# Chapter 34
## Hostages Held and Message Heard

On September 13, 1988, I went to the old movie theater where I had worked and met with one of the employees who wanted to sell his AK-47. He had the gun in his trunk. I purchased it from him for $350. The sale also included six magazines, four of which were fully loaded. I told him that if anything happened, not to say anything.

That night I went to my English class at J. Sargeant Reynolds Community College. I turned in a paper as requested on a bad experience in my life. Of course, it was one of my many war stories.

The class sat stunned as I read. In listening, they were becoming aware of more than they had known of life in Beirut from a headline or two. Most were hearing for the first time how different life was for someone their age living in a country splintered by war. As I finished, they sat silent for a moment and then began to comment on the report. Most admitted that what I reported was not common knowledge among their contemporaries.

Giving the report heightened my desire to do something to make more people aware of how horrible things were in Lebanon. The teacher asked me "What could be done about the situation in Lebanon?" But there was no time to discuss that issue. At that point, I knew I had to do something.

That night, while back in my driveway at home, I checked the AK-47 to make sure that it was working well. I took it apart and made sure it was oiled. Holding it in my hands brought back more painful memories of home and the carnage and destruction there. This AK-47, old reliable, the weapon of choice, simple to take apart and put back together, would help in my quest to make those in the states more aware of what was really going on in the city of Beirut as well as in southern Lebanon.

The next morning, I dressed in jeans and my white Leonardo's Pizza shirt. I headed towards Leonardo's and on the way there, I decided that now was the time to do it, either now or never. I was calm, but thinking deeply of the war and my family. I felt I was on a mission against the Israeli invaders who were occupying southern Lebanon.

Once I got to Tuckernuck Shopping Center where the U.S. Armed Forces Recruiting Center was located, I parked the car and looked around and saw people walking around enjoying the day in this normal U.S. city. Seeing them, I thought of the lifestyle we lived back in Lebanon, always in a hurry, always in survival mode.

I reached in the back seat and grabbed the AK-47. I already had a 25 caliber in my back pocket, which I carried with me most of the time. Once I got the AK-47 into the front seat, I put the magazines in my back pocket. I put a magazine into the AK-47 and chambered the gun, making sure that the safety was off. I had a small towel to cover the gun, but on the way out of the car, I threw the towel on the ground while thinking to myself who is going to say anything to someone carrying an AK-47?

As I crossed the parking lot, two elderly women coming out of the store next to the center looked at me with puzzled expressions. I looked at them, smiled, and kept walking to my destination. They quickly looked away, heading with haste back to their cars with their shopping carts.

I headed toward the recruiting center feeling confident and sure that this would definitely send a message to the Lebanese people that someone really cares about them. I had a strong grip on my gun as I pushed the front door open. It was very quiet except for a few murmurs inside the station. I passed all the service banners hanging inside for the Marines, Army, and Navy.

I reached the first office, which was Navy, where a recruiter was on the telephone. I approached him with my AK-47, pointed it at him and gently said, "Do as I tell you and don't try anything funny unless you want it to be your last day at work."

His eyes widened and he told whoever he was talking to that he would call him back later. I told him that if he did what I told him, he would not be harmed, but to listen to all the details I was going to tell him.

I told him we were going to the next office. The first two offices were small and the third office, the largest, was located in the back of the building.

I told him to go to the second office, the Army office. There were two female soldiers in there and, when the recruiter entered in front of me, he told them not to do anything stupid and to listen to what I had to say. Stunned, they followed my instructions and headed out the office door to the hallway. From there, all three of them walked in front of me to the third office where there were seven people when I only expected there would be one. The look of puzzlement on the faces of the seven when the other recruiters entered changed to concern when they saw me and the AK-47 and knew something was terribly wrong.

I told the two ladies to have a seat in the office chairs and I asked the men to take off their shoes and lie on the ground against the wall. I told them that I was only going to repeat it once, that I was not going to harm anyone as long as they did what I asked them to do.

As I was doing that, an eleventh person walked into the office. I pointed the gun at him and told him to join the rest.

I could feel their fear and see it in their eyes. Since I was in control of the situation, I assured them that there was nothing to worry about, that I was only here to bring attention to the war in Lebanon, and that I loved this country.

I grabbed the American flag that was hanging inside the office and told them that I had nothing against the United States citizens, but I did have a problem with the United States government. I promised them that no one would be harmed as long as they didn't do anything stupid or try to leave. Then, I offered them the coffee and doughnuts which were there in the office.

After saying that, the tensions seemed to ease while I had other things on my mind to deal with. I asked them to lie face down on the floor. Then, I quickly went to the front door of the building and leaned a chair and a large brochure stand against it at an angle so that no matter who opened the door, the chair and the sign would fall and the noise would alert me while I was in the back.

I went back to the third office where everyone was still lying on the ground watching each other, and then me, as I walked into the room. I took eleven bullets out of my pocket and lined them up on the table just to scare them.

I picked up the phone and dialed 911. The operator answered saying "Henrico Police. What is your emergency?" I told the operator that I had taken eleven people hostage at the U.S. Armed Forces Recruiting Center in the Tuckernuck Shopping Center and that they needed to send a hostage negotiator.

After hanging up, I had one of the recruiters call to make sure that the 911 operator did not think it was a joke. I only let him talk to the dispatcher for a few seconds and then I made him hang up the phone. Once that call was made, all the phones in the recruiting station started ringing.

After picking up a few lines, a Henrico officer on one of them asked me if I was the person in charge. I said, "Yes." I told him that I needed to talk with a negotiator and that there were two others working with me there. Then he asked me where I was from and I said, "Beirut, Lebanon." He said that he was working on connecting me with a hostage negotiator but it would take a few minutes. He wanted to talk more, but I told him I would wait for the negotiator's call and hung up.

All the phone lines lit up. I went to a room behind the third office to the main circuit breaker for the building. I cut all the circuit breakers on and off until I found that one that controlled the phones. I shut it off stopping all the phones from ringing. Shutting off the means of communication would put the police more on edge, heightening the crisis. I knew that in a few minutes I would turn it back on.

Now it was very quiet in the office. I stood in the doorway of the room where all the people were so I could see them and still see down the hallway and out into the parking lot.

Seeing the parking lot had been mostly cleared, I went back to the circuit breaker and turned the phones back on. Immediately, they began to ring. I let them ring for a while because one of the recruiters had asked if he could use the restroom. I wanted to make sure that I would not be distracted. Once the recruiter came back from the bathroom and got back on the ground, I picked up the phone and started to talk to the hostage negotiator, my gun still aimed in the general direction of the hostages.

The long phone cord made it possible for me to stand at the office doorway and see the parking lot through the large front window. I gave the negotiator my name and told him when he asked that I had eleven hostages. I gave him their names and told him that they were all safe and would not be released until "our" demands were met. I wanted him to think I was not a lone gunman. I wanted him to understand that if he did not want anyone to get hurt, to make sure no one tried to enter the building. I told him I wanted my statement concerning the situation in Lebanon to be publicized on the TV and on radio station XL102. Once that was done and after discussing it with my "two collaborators," I would release the hostages one at a time.

The negotiator asked if what I wanted was peace in the world, and I told him that this was not a joke, that I was more concerned about the war in Lebanon and also wanted to get my family out of Beirut. He said that had to do with immigration and might take longer.

During the conversation, I could see through the plate glass window that fire trucks had blocked off Broad Street. I could see what appeared to be a SWAT team running around outside. I had my gun aimed in their direction and wondered to myself if they thought their black SWAT outfits made them difficult to see. If they had a sniper team on the roof, I would be fine as long as I stayed where I was standing, because on that angle, they could not see me.

After hearing the first announcement on WRXL-102 on the recruiting station radio, I decided to release one of the female recruiters. I gave her physical description to the negotiator before releasing her. After that, I said I would wait longer until my message got more publicity on the news.

Listening to my plea on the radio brought me great relief. After it became major news I was even happy and didn't care what my consequences would be. Those burdens I had been carrying had been lifted. I could now be the normal Sam that I was before that day. I felt I had done my duty to my country, my friends, and my family. It was over. There would be no reason for me to escalate the situation.

I released the second female hostage after giving her description to the hostage negotiator. I tried to lighten the mood in the recruiting station by asking what kind of music people liked and they seemed to be put at ease and started to joke, knowing that my demands had been met and that I was not going to do any harm to them. But, I still kept one eye on the front hallway and one on the hostages. I also apologized to them about what happened that day, telling them at least they got the day off.

As this was going on, more and more broadcasts were aired on all the FM stations. As the message was getting on the air over many stations, I decided to release the hostages in order according to their military rank, leaving the senior ranking officer last just in case things went south. I also planned to exit the center unarmed. Hopefully, because the media was there, the police would be less likely to fire at an unarmed man.

Many of the hostages wished me well as they exited the office. I smiled and told them I would probably see them in court. I didn't want to shake anybody's hand at the time because I still had a strong grip on my AK-47.

The negotiator on the phone seemed to be happy that things were being resolved. He had taken me seriously and understood that I just wanted to get my message across. The tension eased as I began releasing one hostage every fifteen minutes.

As the last hostage, the highest ranking officer, was released, I loosened my grip on the AK-47 to shake his hand. He understood how I felt about my country and my family and he wished me well as he walked out the front door. I repositioned myself in the recruiting station and had my gun drawn, looking through its sights at the doorway, scanning the parking lot because now I'm sure they know that instead of three hostage takers, there was only one.

There did not seem to be any movement outside. The negotiator asked me to come outside, lay down my weapons, and then go back inside while they retrieved them. I asked how I could walk out with my weapons in my hands and not be shot. He said that if I held the AK-47 upright by its muzzle and placed it on the sidewalk, everything should be fine.

I laid the phone's receiver on the table as I proceeded to take the magazine out of the AK-47 and re-chambered the gun, ejecting the bullet. The gun was now empty and safe. I also took the 25 caliber handgun out of my back pocket and took the magazine out and cleared its chamber. Doing this, I felt a sense of peace. I had no problems facing the consequences. I was actually proud of doing it in a manner where no one was hurt and yet, at the same time, the message was carried across the world. I put the phone receiver back to my ear and told the negotiator that I was preparing to come out and surrender my weapons before retreating back into the building.

I put the receiver back down, grabbed the AK-47 by the muzzle, put the magazines in my back pocket, and carried the 25 caliber pistol by its barrel in my other hand, holding them both out in front of me. I walked to the front door, grasped the door handle with the fingers on the hand carrying the AK-47, and pulled it open. I walked out in front of the glass window of the recruiting station. I tossed the small gun on the ground and then put the magazines down out of my back pocket. I gently placed the AK-47 onto the sidewalk in front of me.

Finally, it was done.

# Chapter 35
## Consequences

The unmarked white van traveled along Parham Road to the Henrico County Court Building, passing through two gates. The front gate was chain link so you could see through it. When they opened up the van's double doors and helped me out, the reporters started clicking pictures rapidly even though it was only a few steps into the building where the detectives wanted to ask a few questions before I went to be fingerprinted.

I said I would as long as I could get McDonald's, a soda, and a pack of Marlboro Reds. Within ten minutes, I was chewing on a McDonald's hamburger and sipping on a Coke. I hadn't eaten all day. I had the cigarettes, too, but no matches. It was a non-smoking facility.

After that, the investigators took me to another room, an office with phones and cubicles. We sat down and the detective started questioning me about what I had just done. I explained it to him the same way I explained it to the negotiator.

He asked why I picked that day and jokingly I replied that the weather was great. He also asked me where I got the guns and I told him the truth. Because I seemed at ease, he seemed to relax. I told him my main concern was my family and trying to get attention to the war in Lebanon.

After we finished the interview, he asked me if I had any more guns. I told him I also had a 22 pistol in my suitcase at the house where I was staying. He then asked if I wanted to make a phone call from the phone at the cubicle. I called Mr. Fahed, the head of the household that had welcomed me as one of their own. Peggy, Fred's wife, answered the phone and sounded as if she had been crying.

She asked me if I was alright and I told her I was sorry for what happened. She gave the phone to Fred who asked "What the hell were you thinking?"

He asked if I was okay and I told him I was. I told him I would talk to him later. He also told me that the FBI had come to his house with a search warrant.

I felt horrible about that. If I had realized that the Fahed family would go through all of that, I would have moved out before any of this happened. I did not want to cause them any grief. They had treated me like their own son. The last thing I wanted to do was hurt them in any way.

He also mentioned that the media was outside their house. I felt sick inside that they were going through this. I wanted to be the only one dealing with this situation, not anyone else.

As the sun was setting, I was escorted by the officers to their unmarked car in the parking lot. There was no media around at the time and no one knew which building I was in at the county complex.

We walked at a normal pace and I was surprised at how relaxed they were with me and that they did not feel the need to rush me to the car.

After getting into the car, we drove around the block to the next building where they said I was going to be booked, fingerprinted, and interviewed by the FBI.

Because there were thirty-seven charges against me, there would have to be thirty-seven sets of fingerprints. I smiled, nodded at them, and said I didn't have any other plans for the evening.

Once we entered the building, it seemed as if all the officers that were in the building wanted to see this kid who had been all over the news. They introduced me to a female officer, a blond, nice-looking lady, who told me this was going to take a long time. She asked that I be patient and cooperate with her. I smiled at her and told her she wouldn't be having any problems with me.

During the fingerprinting process, my hands were covered with ink. While she was fingerprinting me, we exchanged small talk and she asked me if I was the guy who took over the recruiting station. When I said yes, she said that I seemed to be a very nice person and I said, "I am."

I told her the only reason I did it was to bring media attention to my country. She gave me a break for a few minutes and went to answer the phone about two feet away. I could hear her saying on the phone that she was fingerprinting me, adding that she was surprised at what a nice young man I was. After hanging up the phone, she told me that the call was from her daughter who knew her mom was working in that department and would be processing the hostage taker.

After the thirty-seven sets of fingerprints were done, the officer directed me to a sink with special soap for removing the ink from my hands. Then, I was taken into a holding tank which looked like an aquarium with a large rectangular glass window making it easy for the guards to observe inside.

The room measured about 8' x 10' and already had six people in there when I entered. No one knew who I was. There was a drunken man puking in the toilet in the far left corner. There were two bunk beds along one wall and a single cot by the window. One person was on the wall phone, crying while talking to his wife because he wanted her to bail him out. He told her he was stuck in a hell hole.

I lay down on the bunk closest to the glass window while exchanging small talk with my new neighbors. After telling them why I was in there, the room got very quiet so I decided to get some sleep as I was exhausted.

I could still see other guards peeking in the window and pointing. More guards came, looking through the glass at us. I felt like we were in the zoo and they weren't feeding the animals. After thirty minutes of deep sleep, I was awakened by a guard. He asked that I follow him to be interviewed by the FBI.

The guard that escorted me was a very heavy-set fellow with reddish hair. After going through a few security doors where we had to be buzzed in and a few hallways, I began to feel the way my hamsters must have felt in their aquarium-like cage.

The office where the FBI agents were awaiting me had a door with a vertical rectangular window. I could see them sitting around a large oval table as I entered. They were nicely dressed in business suits and were clean-shaven. As I entered the room, two FBI agents shook my hand and asked me to have a seat at the head of the table. The two Henrico County detectives that had interviewed me that morning were also present. Each had a brief case and a few folders on the table. They proceeded to ask me my name and if I wanted to cooperate and give my testimony to them.

I thought to myself that it was better to be in this room with them than in the aquarium I had just left. I felt at ease because I had accomplished what I set out to do: bring attention to the devastating war in Lebanon. I had nothing to hide. That was all I wanted, that and to get my family out of there and into the states.

They asked me why I did what I did and why I picked the recruiting station. Was I in contact with anyone from overseas? Was I coerced into doing this? When I answered no to both, they seemed surprised. At first, it seemed that they didn't believe me because I had picked a military target and also because I used a Russian-made AK-47.

They also asked me why I made them take their shoes off. I said for two reasons: one, most of the time people in public places feel uncomfortable with their shoes off and secondly, if anyone was to run, it would be difficult to get away quickly in their sock feet as the office floor was slick with wax.

The FBI looked surprised when I said that. I told them I picked the recruiting station because I was sure it would get the greater media coverage as the hostages were military personnel.

One of the FBI agents asked repeatedly if I was connected to Hezbollah or any other Lebanese faction. I got annoyed with him and looked him in the eye and told him that if he asked one more stupid question like that, I was going to end the interview. I also said that I take full responsibility for all my actions and they could do to me whatever they wanted. This caused them to soften their approach a bit.

Later on, they opened up a briefcase which contained a folder of photographs. Could I identify certain individuals among the 8 x 10 headshots of bearded men? Also, there was a close up photo of a man wearing a Red Cross uniform picking through the rubble of what looked like a car bomb in Beirut.

After looking at the photos, I told them that I didn't recognize any of them, which was the truth. I thought to myself that I would not identify any of them even if I did know who they were because they had put me in the same category as the men in the photos.

I would not want to endanger my family or my country by revealing an identity that they might pursue and my family might suffer because of it. They also asked me about an Armenian man who had the same last name as my mother's maiden name. They were persistent in their questions about him. Years later, it came to light that he had close ties to the Clinton administration, having visited the White House six or more times. His name was Mourad Topalian, an American of Armenian descent, who was later charged in 1999 with acts of conspiracy and terrorism and possessing and storing explosives and firearms. His underlying motive for these acts was to draw attention to the Armenian genocide at the hands of the Turks.

They asked me at the end of the interview if there was anything else that I needed to add to my statement. During the whole interview, I was aware of them writing down as well as recording the interview. After I told them that I had given them all the information I had, I said that they could come and get me from my cell if they had any other questions later. They shook my hand and gave me their cards which I later flushed down the toilet.

Once I was escorted back to the holding tank/aquarium, a new detainee recognized me from the TV and high-fived me and asked me if I could talk to his sister on the phone. She had been telling him that it was all over the news and she wanted my autograph. Once the other detainees heard this conversation, they all got excited when they found out that I was now a celebrity of sorts. I talked to the sister on the phone and she asked if I would be her pen pal.

A clean-cut African American with a nice shirt and slacks entered our holding tank and to our surprise, we found out that he still had a pack of cigarettes in his shirt pocket. Normally, it would have been confiscated. Those of us who smoked really needed a cigarette which he was happy to provide as he also looked a little frightened by all of us. We held the cigarettes below the window level so they couldn't see us through the glass. To conserve the cigarettes, we decided to pass one around to several people.

As we were smoking, a new detainee entered the office outside our window. He started getting loud with the lady taking his information and using vulgar language. As he got louder, he was surrounded by five correctional officers who threw him on the ground and handcuffed him.

In the scuffle, his shirt was torn and his mouth was bleeding. They tried to put him in our holding tank and we all said no because we were at capacity with folks sitting on the floor. They reconsidered and put him in the cell adjacent to us. The struggle with the guards was an entertaining diversion as we waited to see what was going to happen to us.

Two of the drunks made bail during the night. Now sober, they said goodbye and good luck to us as they left. There was not a boring moment all night as people came and went from the tank as business was booming.

# Chapter 36
## Dayroom #27 - Henrico County Jail

The next morning, after our breakfast was delivered in Styrofoam boxes along with a cup of coffee, we went to processing where jail uniforms were given: light brown scrubs and flip-flops. We turned in our civilian clothes, mine being my white Leonardo's Pizza shirt and my severely faded jeans. I also had $200 in my pocket which was added to my canteen account.

After that, we were escorted upstairs to the main jail which the inmates called the zoo. We walked through a long, very clean hallway with cameras mounted near the ceiling. We were buzzed through several doors, past the kitchen, and down another hallway to dayrooms or open areas for community leisure activities adjacent to individual cells.

There were people with their arms hanging out of the bars asking if you had anything to give them, whether it was your shoes or anything of value. I ignored them and kept walking behind the corrections officer. A few guys recognized me from the TV and were telling other inmates what I had done. After all that chaos with people yelling, whistling, and shouting, we finally made it to dayroom #27 which was much quieter.

The officer took a large key from his key ring and opened up a control box outside the dayroom and buzzed us through two sets of doors, the second door not opening until the first was completely shut. We each had a pillow which was about as comfortable as a sandbag.

Once in the dayroom, we saw people playing cards at one table, checkers at another, with the TV blaring and some looking down over the railing of the second tier of cells as we came in.

The guard escorted me to my assigned cell and there was already one guy in there by the name of Larry. He was a Caucasian male with a long beard and a long mullet. He was happy to have a roommate because it was boring to be in there alone. He already knew who I was from the TV. I smiled and said, "I guess I get the top bunk." He said either was fine with him. I told him that as a kid I always wanted a bunk bed and would be happy to take the top bunk.

The officer had me sign a paper checking off the condition of the cell, its walls, floor, etc. On the right wall, there were drawings of beautiful mermaids along with some dark, satanic looking pictures done in pencil. All were life-size with great detail. Inmates from long ago had put their names and dates of confinement here and there on the wall, something I had seen in movies about prison life.

One thing that grabbed my attention and made me smile was where someone had marked his time using six slash marks with a seventh across each set of six to indicate a week of confinement. I started to do it but realized that I would probably be there much longer and needed to mark off months, rather than weeks.

I decided to take a shower because I hadn't showered in two days and smelled like a billy goat. There was only one and it had a big glass window. I opened the door and looked in and saw how filthy it was. I asked the inmate/trusty assigned to our dayroom for cleaning supplies. He gave me a bottle of cleanser and a long scrub brush. I used the entire bottle to clean the shower.

When he said I was using too much cleanser, I told him that I was going to clean the shower the way it should be cleaned. He never said anything after that. I told him that I would probably be spending a lot more time in this jail than he was. All the detainees in dayroom #27 combined would probably serve less time than I would as I was facing multiple felonies.

After showering, I felt like a newborn again.

We were advised by the guards about sick call in the morning. If anyone had an illness or anything needing medical attention, he had to put his name on the list.

In the morning, a guard yelled "Chow time!" Everybody hopped to their feet and lined up waiting for the guard to buzz us through to the mess hall.

On the way there, inmates were waving and wanting to pass notes to other inmates. Some acted as runners delivering notes and packs of cigarettes from one inmate to another without the guards seeing them.

Once we got to the mess hall, there was a long line to pick up plastic trays and what looked like food was scooped directly into one of the tray compartments. The only thing I recognized was the toast and the small carton of milk. The rest was mystery meat and powdered eggs.

After lining up on the stainless steel seats, inmates from other dayrooms started to join us except for one guy holding up a sign made out of cardboard which said, "Free Mandela!"

A few words were exchanged between him and people sitting next to me. Finally, an African-American stood up and said, "The hell with Mandela. Who is going to free us?" He then tossed a piece of toast at the guy with the sign. He kept waving his sign side to side and kept yelling "Free Mandela, free Mandela" while everyone laughed. More threw food at him and one guy standing behind the sign bearer took the sign away and threw it on the ground, starting the first fight of the day in the mess hall.

Inmates took advantage of the situation by tossing any food they didn't want in their direction. There were plastic cups and hash browns all over the wall and all the correctional officers were called into the mess hall. They took the Mandela supporter and the guy who took his sign, handcuffed them both, and took them to isolation.

After eating, we pushed our trays to the dishwasher through a window with an overhead pull-down door. There was a big trash bucket outside the window where we first banged our trays to clean them before handing them to the dishwasher. He loaded the trays into a crate and sprayed them to loosen up the food. He then slid them onto the dishwasher track where a jet of hot water and soap sprayed the trays as if they were cars going through a carwash.

The first week in jail was a constant parade of lawyers, FBI agents, detectives, and some visitors, mainly my American family and friends from Leonardo's. The Fahed family had contacted my parents and informed them of what had happened even though it had been on the news in Beirut. My parents had seen the news story but because they had company, they didn't notice it was their son who was the hostage taker on TV. The next day I was told it was in all the papers and on the TV in Lebanon.

My parents had to get permission from the American Consulate to travel to the U.S. They first flew to the United Arab Emirates and then to Washington, D.C. They were escorted off the plane by FBI agents who questioned them. My cousin, the one I initially lived with when I came to the U.S., drove my parents to Richmond to see me. He never visited me or came to court to testify in my behalf out of embarrassment and fear that it might jeopardize his work.

My first meeting with my parents was from behind a glass window using a phone. The sad look on my mother's face was heart-wrenching. I tried to stay composed by telling them that I was doing well and that I already had an attorney that my cousin had chosen for me. I was glad to see my little brother Dani. His face was sad and his jaw clenched as he looked at the cops because he thought they were the ones who put me in there. An extended visit was allowed with my family only after my attorneys obtained permission from the jail captain and only because they had come from out of the country.

My parents, who had already met with the attorney my cousin suggested, asked if I had met with him. It wasn't until a few days after my parents' visit that I actually did.

On that day, I was called out of my cell into a room where a man wearing a navy blue suit was sitting at a desk. He was neatly dressed, his beard was neatly trimmed, and his blonde hair was combed smoothly across his forehead. He asked me to tell him in detail what had occurred at the recruiting station and suggested that I keep my voice low in case there might be listening devices in the room. He asked me to write everything that had happened down on a legal pad. He would work with the county on setting a date to go before the judge to set bail and schedule a court date.

Eventually, bail was set at $250,000 and a court date was scheduled six months from that day. I, however, remained in jail. In those six months, I was to be evaluated by a private psychiatrist and then a state psychiatrist. I met with my attorney several times to discuss my case.

While waiting for my court date, I spent time watching TV in the dayroom. We always voted on which channel to watch. One day, a younger kid who looked like he belonged in a juvenile facility instead of a jail, changed the channel in the middle of a program, creating anger and frustration among the viewers.

I went to the TV and changed it back to what we were watching. The kid said he was going to change it again. I told him he could change it to any other channel he wanted to while I stood by the TV.

The TV was sitting on a low table and as he walked towards the TV to change the channel, I thought to myself what do I have to lose? I am facing 250 years in prison so I have nothing to lose.

When the kid bent down to change the channel, I swung my fist as hard as I could, my fist landing squarely on his jaw. He stumbled and fell to the ground, then tried to stand back up but his feet were wobbly as I had caught him off guard. Everybody jumped between us to stop the fight which I wouldn't call a fight because he wasn't fighting back. People in the background were yelling, "That's what you get for trying to mess with the TV."

Since all those in the dayroom were long timers, they all approved of my actions against the kid, a newcomer, who wanted to be in charge of the TV. In a few minutes, the guards were in the dayroom and the others were defending me saying that the kid started it. But, since I had no visible wounds and I had thrown the first punch, the guards escorted me to isolation on the third floor. I had to put all my belongings, such as my legal pad, stamps, and mail, the most important of my belongings, in a black trash bag along with my sandbag of a pillow. On the way to isolation, we had to stop at the medical department for the nurse to fill out a report concerning the fight and to make sure I was okay before I went into isolation.

# Chapter 37
## Isolation

On the way to the third floor isolation, I passed some dayrooms where my fellow inmates yelled words of encouragement because they saw where I was headed. There were two sets of steel doors to go through to get to isolation. Once the doors were shut behind me, you could hardly hear any noises.

There were about seven isolation cells, but only two were occupied. I was the third guest. I noticed a small shower in the hallway going towards my cell and a blue phone on the wall. I also noticed a camera that covered the narrow hallway. I could see the slots on the steel doors where food or mail could be passed through. The door contained an open barred square at eye-level.

The guard opened the isolation cell door with a huge key and as I walked into my new apartment, I could see the standard stainless steel sink and a stainless steel toilet, known for its powerful flush.

It reminded me of a time in the dayroom where an inmate held on to one end of a large plastic bag while flushing the other end. He had to pull back with both hands on the bag to keep it from going down. When I asked him what he was doing, he smiled at me with his gold teeth and said, "I'm fishing."

Everyone laughed because it looked as if there could be a huge fish fighting him on the other end. So, I had to try it myself to believe him. It was not as easy as dynamiting the fish in Beirut.

Once the officer checked the cell and was locking the door, he looked in and said, "I hope you can do these two weeks in isolation."

I responded by saying "I could do my time in a corner of a matchbox.

He laughed and said, "See you in two weeks."

I yelled back, "When can I take a shower?"

He replied, "In isolation, every Tuesday and Friday."

Once the officer was gone through those two steel doors, the other two inmates started to yell. While I was talking to them about why I was in there, I realized that the officer forgot to confiscate my cigarettes. I had two full packs of Marlboro Reds and a book of matches. Once I told the other two that I had the cigarettes, they started to laugh and bang on the door with joy.

I took one cigarette and tossed it toward the cell adjacent to mine. The inmate used his legal pad and a shoestring to fish the cigarette under the door. After a few tries, he was successful. Then I tossed a few more to him so that he could toss them to the cell next to him. We continued to smoke and talk to each other through the small door openings.

I found out that the inmate in the first cell, who had a huge Afro, was a homeless person. When I asked how he ended up in here, he answered, "By choice."

I asked him to explain what he meant by "choice." He said every year when the weather got cold he would stand in front of a store window and toss a brick through it and then wait for the cops to come and arrest him. He has done it so many times that the judge easily recognizes him when he comes in.

After hearing that, the other inmate and I started to laugh. The other inmate said he was also in there for fighting in the jail over someone cheating at a card game. He said that he recognized me from TV and that at least I had the heart to do what I did and to say that I did it myself since everybody else in prison either said they didn't do it, they were framed, or it was the white man's fault, something I heard all the time. I heard it so much I started saying it myself.

After a long night of talking and smoking, I decided to ration the cigarettes and made sure to smoke them after count had been taken so the officer would not detect the smell.

The light in the cell stayed on constantly, even during the night, making sleep difficult. I decided to use my sandbag pillow as a battering ram and kept hitting the light, something that had been suggested to me by the inmate next door. After twenty or more tries and being exhausted from jumping up and down and swinging at the light, it finally went out. Then I was able to sleep better at night.

In the morning we were awakened by the words, "Chow time!" when an inmate dressed in white peeped through my window, opened up the slot, and handed me my breakfast in a Styrofoam container followed by a small Styrofoam cup of coffee.

He smiled and asked all of us how we were doing. We all laughed and said we loved it back there. Within minutes they were gone and it was back to quiet.

After eating breakfast, the count was taken and we started smoking our cigarettes again. The two guys thanked me numerous times for the cigarettes as it made isolation much more pleasant, especially for us smokers.

Then I introduced them to fishing in the toilet. Since all of us had the big black trash bags we brought into isolation with us, you could hear the loud flushing noises of all three cells followed by giggling.

After a few hours of fishing in the toilet, the homeless guy yelled over and said that he wondered what the jail's water bill would be like. The other inmate laughed saying that our families' taxes were paying for it anyway.

The next day was shower day, so we did push-ups and sit-ups for hours until we were exhausted and sweaty and looking forward to a warm shower.

That morning, the officer asked who wanted to take showers. My next-door neighbor and I accepted, but the homeless man didn't want anything to do with the shower. My neighbor went first and he told me he was going to take his time as the guards would take their time returning.

I thought I would give him some cigarettes while he was out of his cell rather than him having to fish along the floor for them. I put them in an envelope to disguise them from the hall camera. He gave some to the homeless man making sure his back was to the camera as he passed by his cell.

After finishing his shower, which took about a half an hour, he waited in the hall for the guard to come back. Once the guard returned, it was my turn to go. It was the best feeling to sit under the water for about 45 minutes. The shower had a small window that looked out onto the dayrooms. I banged on the window a few times until I got the attention of someone in the dayroom who knew me. I had to yell very loud because it was almost soundproof in isolation. I asked them to send us some cigarettes if it was possible. He yelled back he would see what he could do.

After going back into my cell, the guard thought that I had closed my door and didn't realize that it was slightly ajar. After the guard left, I ran up and down the hallway. Finally, a loud noise came from the intercom as they had seen me on camera. I went up to the camera and gave them the finger. So did the other two inmates, sticking their arms through the square in the door. The guard got agitated and said that if I didn't slam my door shut, he was going to send a guard up there to do it for me and make me stay in isolation longer.

So after an hour of running around the hall and even using the phone, I went back into my cell and slammed the door shut behind me. The guard responded, "Thank you!"

After the two weeks were up, I realized how hard isolation or being caged could be on an animal, let alone a human being. From then on, I promised myself that I would never put a dog or a bird in a cage. I could imagine how hard it would be to spend a lifetime in a cage the way some animals, like Ahmed the parrot, were made to live.

On being released from isolation, I said goodbye to my two new friends who remained behind. I would probably see them again if only in the mess hall and we could pick up our conversations where we left off.

# Chapter 38
## Kitchen Whites

Once back in dayroom #27, I was greeted by my fellow inmates who were happy to see me back among them. After taking a nap in my cell, I was awakened by other inmates telling me that I was on the 6:00 evening news. They watched it with me as the announcer said my court date had been set for the trial.

Soon after, I applied for a job in the kitchen, one no one thought I would get after taking eleven people hostage and spending time in solitary for fighting. Every time I went through the chow line and saw the lady that ran the kitchen, Miss Betty, with her gold teeth and her designer DK glasses, I would mention to her that I was interested in working in the kitchen as I had previously worked as a cook at Leonardo's Pizza. She was a tough woman, who had been raised in Church Hill, a rough neighborhood in Richmond at the time she was growing up, and always kept a big wooden spatula close by in case an inmate threw his food back at her or threatened her in any manner.

To everyone's surprise, one day I got a notice saying that I was approved to work in the kitchen. Other inmates were upset because they had applied for the job before I did and were not chosen. Immediately I was moved from dayroom #27 to a dayroom by the kitchen that was for trusties only. Those included kitchen workers who scrubbed pots and pans, prepared food, readied tables, served Kool-Aid, scraped and washed trays, and best of all, delivered food on a cart to those in isolation, those in the drunk tank, as well as those in the court building.

Also living there were those who worked in the barber shop, the laundry, or swept floors.

This was a much better environment because everybody worked and no one wanted to get in trouble because if they did, they would lose their jobs and go back to living in the zoo. My roommate was also a kitchen worker and seemed to be very nice. He only had six months left before he would be released. He said the cool thing about working in the kitchen was that you would get to see the female inmates we had never seen because they ate at a different time from the male inmates. He said you could pass notes to them as long as the guard didn't see you. If caught, you could lose your job.

I was handed my kitchen whites and my apron and was actually excited to start cleaning the pots and pans, the hardest job in the kitchen. They said most people couldn't last more than a week. But, I guess they didn't know how hyperactive I was, and now that I knew that I was going to get twice the amount of food, I was more motivated and washed every pot and pan without any problems. When my station was inspected, it was always spotless, something they rarely saw.

I also learned that there was a lot of food smuggled from the kitchen. I was asked if I wanted to participate because the food was shared in the trusty dayroom and I agreed. I put some chicken sandwiches wrapped in saran wrap in a trash can outside the kitchen door and later, after I was patted down before returning to my cell, I picked up the sandwiches and handed them to another inmate through the bars.

After evening roll call, we had our feast of food that only kitchen workers could access. If you needed cigarettes, you could sell a sandwich for four packs of Newports, the most expensive cigarettes to have in jail.

The trusty area was much calmer than the zoo. People were on their best behavior because any violation would cause permanent loss of status. It meant going back to the regular dayroom where all you could do was play cards and watch TV.

Once I started in the kitchen, the days went by much faster as I was busy cleaning pots and pans. Luckily, I was only on pots and pans for a week because another kitchen worker's transfer to another prison opened up a spot for me. It was the best job in the kitchen though none of the other inmates realized it.

The job called for loading up a chest-high aluminum gray cart with multiple large serving trays of food packaged in Styrofoam boxes, the trays sliding in and out of the cart's tracks. The deputy would call the courthouse and ask them how many prisoners were waiting for court. He would also call isolation to see how many people there needed food. Once all the numbers were confirmed, Miss Betty ordered the guys on the line to fill Styrofoam trays with food while I prepared the drinks, putting lids on all the drinks in case we hit a bump during delivery. I learned to put two extra trays of food on the cart in case a mistake was made in the count, which happened more than once.

My first day with the delivery job I got to go all over the place: isolation on the third floor, receiving on the first floor where the aquarium was, and the courthouse where inmates awaited trial. The courthouse jail was only accessible by going through a long tunnel-like hallway. It had only two doors with cameras at each end.

Once we went through the hallway and entered the courthouse jail, it looked like what you see in the movies. There was an officer at a desk and bars lined one of the walls creating a large holding area for multiple guests. There were separate cells also for individuals who either did not want to be mixed with the others or could not be mixed with the others. The bars had chipped paint, paint that was worn off from salty hands that had grasped them.

Most of the time, the court cell was full of people, some in suits, some in jeans and t-shirts, and some in jail-issued smocks. The atmosphere was always tense and you could see people praying, people sweating, and people who appeared not to care about what was happening. Others were talking about each other's cases, giving each other advice. Some were nervous and silent because nobody really knew what the outcome would be. All of their fates were in the hands of the judge. Some wished others good luck in court as they left the cell for court.

Before leaving the cell, each inmate would have to stick his hands out through a hole while the deputy put handcuffs on them. Once the cuffs were on, he would unlock the cell with the same large key ring full of enormous keys like the ones you always see in the movies.

Walking through those areas, you could feel the heightened tension and you could see those who had already been sentenced. They were either quiet and accepting of their sentences or belligerent and angry because they had gotten longer sentences than they thought they would. Sometimes they would take the tray from me and throw it up against the wall in anger or frustration. There would be no replacement for that tray and I moved on. But I always knew that I would one day be in those cells preparing to go to court and now, at least, I knew what to expect. It gave me a sense of comfort about what was to come.

The officer that was assigned to me and the cart was an older African-American man who would sing some of the most bizarre songs and then laugh and giggle at himself. He gave me instructions not to pass any notes to inmates or get involved in any kind of communication if I wanted to keep my job. So, I smiled and said, "Yes, sir."

Once I figured out that he hardly paid any attention to me, I felt I could get away with a lot more things. As long as the cart was fully supplied and also had condiments like salt and pepper packets, catsup, mustard and all was in order, he didn't care about anything else. He would sing up and down the hallways and even in isolation while the inmates would yell to him to please stop singing. Soon I was comfortable with the duties of my job and knew all the ins and outs as well as the timing as to when we would be in certain places.

After visiting isolation several times, two of the guys there felt comfortable enough to gesture to me through the door about cigarettes. I winked at them unseen by the serenading officer to let them know that I would take care of them.

The next time I came, they were at their windows waiting. I hid five cigarettes in each of the trays while I was in the elevator and the officer was talking on his walkie-talkie. I acted as if I was checking the condiments and the count of the trays to make sure we had enough and knew how to mark the trays to show which ones would go to isolation. By pressing my nails on the corner of the Styrofoam, I marked them inconspicuously and the adventures started.

The people in isolation smiled when they saw me coming and were so happy to be getting a tobacco supply that they even complimented the officer on his singing. The officer said that everyone must feel comfortable with me because the deliveries were going so smoothly.

The most entertaining part was going to receiving where new arrests, still in their street clothes, were readied for the aquarium. Of course, there was also the token number of drunks each time. Some were yelling and screaming at the officers and were so intoxicated that they did not realize they were in a jail until the next morning.

A few guys asked me for cigarettes in the aquarium where no smoking was allowed. I asked them if they would trade me their watches for a few packs of cigarettes because if I got caught, I would lose my job.

After two days of them waiting, they wanted the cigarettes so badly that they traded their watches for two packs apiece. I turned around and sold the watches for two cartons of cigarettes.

Also, I was passing notes from isolation to different dayrooms. On days that a different officer accompanied me, which was rare, I did not do anything to arouse suspicion.

One morning, the drug dogs were brought in. The dog smelled marijuana in one of the cells and sat down there as a signal to the officers that this was the place. The officers searched the room inside and out and found nothing because it must have been smoked the night before. They took all of us downstairs to the aquarium area to get urine samples from us. Two people were removed as trusties after THC was found in their urine.

After that incident, every one of us inmates was on high alert when it came to smuggling things even though the marijuana was brought in by a female officer who usually worked at the Richmond City Jail. She happened to notice one of the trusties who was a good friend of hers in the outside world and would small talk here and there with him. He asked her in a quiet voice while count was being taken if she could bring him some weed. She nodded and two days later, when they came to do the count, she pulled it out of her pocket as she was checking his room and tossed the bag of weed onto his bed and walked away.

That night, everyone could smell the weed. That was when the guards got suspicious and the dogs were brought in. The guys who failed the urine test were put in isolation under strict watch so I didn't even think to attempt to pass them anything, not even a cigarette.

After work each day, I occupied myself by writing letters, having visits with my attorneys or the FBI, and reading my mail. A lot of inmates got little to no mail. I knew I had mail because I could smell the perfume coming from the hallway as the guard delivered the mail. All the inmates wanted to smell my letters and I jokingly told them they could for a few cigarettes. Reading letters from the outside kept me in high spirits and helped me escape jail life briefly.

Family visits were also important. One day, I asked Captain Sutton for an extended visitation with my family since my dad was in town and that only happened about twice a year. I was happy to see my family as usual, but I noticed a strained look on my mother's face. She looked angry, disappointed, and surprised all at the same time. I asked her what was bothering her when she replied, "I can't believe that you were selling guns to teachers at school back in Beirut."

My first reaction was an "I don't know what you are talking about" look on my face. Then, she mentioned the teacher's name, June Tamim. Hearing that name took me back to the day that I showed Ms. Tamim the pearl-handled 25 caliber pistol.

I smiled slightly and gave an explanation. My words were, "But, Mom, she needed protection."

My mom asked, "From what?"

And I reminded her that they were kidnapping Americans at the time. I felt I had done the right thing whether my mother thought it was right or wrong. I asked my mother how she knew and she replied that she had visited Ms. June in Beirut when she was struggling with cancer and that was when she told my mom what a good boy I was and how I had helped her get a gun for her protection.

Sadly, Ms. June passed away not long after my mother's visit.

# Chapter 39
## Life and Death Decisions

After speaking with other inmates about my case and my attorney, I discovered that he had said little as their defense attorney and, consequently, they were all convicted. This is the attorney that my cousin chose for me. I had no say in the choice at the time.

When I met with him, he told me that if I pled guilty, I would get forty-two years on the gun charges plus whatever the judge decided on the abduction charges.

I was devastated and when I went back to the trusty area, I made a collect call to my mother and told her what I had heard about the attorney and what he was offering me. I asked her to get me another attorney even if he was Syrian.

Thankfully, she agreed and two days later, one of the guards said I had a visitor in the attorney visitation rooms. He wasn't Syrian, thankfully, but Jewish, a brilliant and highly respected attorney, Mr. Murray Janus. He was dressed in a nice suit and I was almost blinded by his highly polished gold Rolex with a few diamonds on its face.

He smiled and gave me a firm handshake. On his right wrist, as I shook his hand, I saw a thick gold bracelet. He was very specific and clear in his questions and was very attentive to my replies. He suggested that I not talk to any reporters who wanted to interview me and not discuss anything that we discussed unless it was something that was already known by the public.

Even though we kept the other attorney on board, I felt more comfortable because Mr. Janus was the one in charge.

After meeting with him and feeling better about having such a strong and competent defense attorney, I called my mother, again collect, and thanked her for finding Mr. Janus. She was happy that someone of that caliber was now handling my case.

As the court date got closer, Mr. Janus sat with me one day and discussed the case in great detail. It was my decision to either have a judge or a jury trial or take a plea bargain. I asked him to work on the plea bargain and the results he came up with were much better than what the first attorney had suggested. Also in the mix were the psychiatric and psychological evaluations which all pointed to Post Traumatic Stress Disorder or PTSD.

After a few weeks of his negotiations with Mr. James Gilmore, III, the prosecuting attorney for Henrico County, the only plea bargain I could get was fourteen years for the guns plus whatever the judge decided on the abduction charges. My attorney also recommended that I keep a low profile while in jail, to have no violations, infractions, or confrontations with other inmates or jail officials. He said I should keep my job which would show that I was responsible and not a violent person but one who was entrusted to work around knives and other cooking equipment.

The next morning when I went to work, we went to isolation and I took the trays out of the cart and moved toward the cells. There were three people that day in isolation. When I got to the last cell and looked through the door, I saw a large pool of blood in the middle of the floor and a white inmate lying in his bed with his arm extended over its edge, blood dripping down onto the floor.

I noticed a large staple, like the ones that held together the note pads we were allowed to have in jail. It had been sharpened and used to cut his wrist. I quickly yelled to the guard, stopping his singing. He listened to what I was yelling at him. He got very nervous and tried to call on his radio while at the same time trying to unlock the door. He was not getting a response either because his battery was low or the area we were in was out of range. He asked me to give him a hand and I said the easiest way to get him out of there without getting any blood on us was to use the blanket, put the bloody inmate on it, and slide him across the tile floor.

I started to drag the inmate down the hallway while the officer went ahead of me to unlock doors. We couldn't get an elevator to come up to that floor quickly enough so we had to get buzzed through the stairwell doors. They could see us on the cameras.

Finally, he got somebody on the radio and told them we were on the way to the medical department on the first floor near the aquarium. I pulled the blanket holding the inmate down the stairs, his head hitting every step on the way down.

The guard said, "What are you doing?"

I replied, "If you are not going to give me a hand, this will continue to happen. Could you support his head?"

He shook his head and said that the guy was going to kill himself anyway so let's just keep going. He did try a few times to hold the back end of the blanket to support the inmate's head while talking on his walkie-talkie. It didn't help that much as we were in a great hurry.

We finally made it to the medical department where the nurses put pressure on his wound and asked us how we found him. We repeated to her what had happened and we also found, to our surprise, a note sticking out of his front pocket that mentioned something about not getting enough medical attention.

The nurse immediately took the note away so I could not finish reading it and she wouldn't let the officer read it either. I told the nurse she might need to check the back of his head as it was bumped a few times coming down the stairs. After that, the officer had to file a report on the incident which benefitted me in that it showed me in a compassionate light, even though in transporting the inmate hurriedly, he suffered some bruises on the back of his head.

There were many incidents of people attempting to kill themselves, but especially during holidays. One guy in dayroom #27 dove off the second tier head first, using both of his arms as brakes. He broke both wrists and the inmates joked asking him how he was going to tend to himself when he went to the bathroom.

He later tried to hang himself with a sheet, once again jumping from the second tier. But to his disappointment, the sheet tore. He was very angry that he wasn't successful in killing himself. Because of these attempts, he was put in a padded room down near the aquarium.

Another occupant of that room was a Vietnam vet, who also threatened the guards and would throw his tray against the wall regularly.

When I asked him what his problem was, he said he was a Vietnam vet to which I replied, "Big deal. I grew up in Beirut."

After that, we became buddies and he would not throw his tray anymore. After a few weeks, he was transferred to Central State Mental Hospital, where I had gone for evaluation.

What a terrible place that was. The building was old and held many psychotic patients, some who were inmates. Some had been convicted of brutal murders; some had even dismembered people. I was glad that I was only visiting and after hearing the barbaric stories from the guard, I promised him that I would not feed the animals once inside.

The head psychiatrist there asked the guard to remove my handcuffs making it more comfortable for me to sit and talk with him. His office was like any other doctor's office, not like a prison office.

We discussed my childhood, the war, and what I was thinking about prior to entering the recruiting station. After a few hours, he shook my hand and the guard put the handcuffs back on. The handcuffs were linked to a heavy chain that encircled my waist and connected to a chain that reached my ankles, both of which were cuffed. In jail, when shackled like this, we were said to be doing the "chicken walk" because you could only take short deliberate steps while walking.

After preparing for my case with Mr. Janus, my attorney, he said it was up to me to decide whether or not I wanted to take a plea bargain or face a jury. He said the only thing about going before the jury was that a guilty verdict would give me a longer sentence than a plea bargain. The first attorney I saw said a plea bargain would mean forty-two years for the gun charges alone and the judge would decide time for the abduction charges. Mr. Janus had been able to lower the possible term for the gun charges to fourteen years and again, whatever the judge would decide for the abduction charges. I decided to take the plea bargain and take my chances with the judge.

On the day of the trial, the news media descended on the courthouse. There were reporters inside and out and everyone was talking about the case. My attorney asked me to shave my beard and have a suit sent to me for the day in court and my parents provided that for me. I was confident about my case because Mr. Janus was one of the best attorneys in Virginia. In my mind, at least, I was giving it my best shot.

There were many character witnesses who came to my defense, including my college English professor, Ms. Willis, a chaplain from the jail that knew me well, psychiatrists and psychologists, some private and some court-appointed. As I was walking towards the courtroom, I saw an officer whispering in the judge's ear and then they both turned and looked at me as I got closer.

Once we entered the courtroom, everyone stood up. I could see my parents, some friends, and my young, attractive college professor, at whom I winked. She smiled back at me. My family, mom, dad, and Wess, were all dressed nicely. It seemed like everybody in the courtroom was looking at my family and seemed surprised at how nicely they were dressed. I think they were expecting that someone from Lebanon would be dressed in long robes, the men sporting beards, their camels parked in front of the courthouse.

Once the court was in session, many witnesses came to the stand including some of the recruiters that I held hostage. One of them even recalled that I treated them nicely and that I had expressed my love for this country and its flag.

There was also a videotape that was sent from Lebanon with all the war documentation showing scenes of car bombs, suicide attacks, and the firing of the battleship USS New Jersey onto Lebanese territories. Also, there was footage of the carnage at the massacres at Sabra and Shatila. The judge would not allow the tapes of the massacre to be shown. At that, I wondered if the judge had already made up his mind when he would not allow them to be shown as part of my defense.

After the deliberations were over, the judge asked me if I had anything to say. I stood up and told them that I was sorry for my actions and that I did not mean to hurt anyone.

After that I sat down and the judge began reading the charges. I had only pled guilty to four firearms charges as part of the plea bargain. For the abduction, I pled guilty to all eleven charges. The judge sentenced me to one hundred and twenty-four years with ninety-nine suspended, leaving me with twenty-five years on all the charges, the time to be served concurrently.

I was relieved, somewhat, but was wondering why he didn't give me a lesser sentence because of all the evidence and the determination of PTSD. But, I knew that they wanted to make an example of me since I caused so much chaos and had garnered both national and international attention. Also, having a twenty-year-old take over a military recruiting station was embarrassing for the military.

I looked at my family and they looked both shocked and distraught at the sentence I was given. I waved at them as I was escorted back into the jail where everyone already knew my fate because it had been announced on the TV.

Before going to my dayroom, I was taken to the visitation room where I could see my parents through the glass window. My parents told me to keep my chin up and do what I had to do. I was mentally and physically exhausted, so when I went back to my dayroom, I slept for an hour.

My mother was always supportive of me in good times and bad. However, I was never quite sure how my dad would react to any given situation. On the one hand, he would arrive in a jeep with gun-wielding militia to rescue me from school when the bombs fell, but on the other, he would ignore my mom's plea to send me to a good school because he felt I would not make anything of myself and might as well get a job. To my surprise, after I was sent to the penitentiary, he wrote the following letter to Dr. Salim El-Hoss, then Prime Minister of Lebanon:

*Dear Dr. Salim El-Hoss:*

*I am well aware that you are busy with the affairs of State, but I am compelled to turn to you for help in resolving a crisis in my family as a result of the war.*

*My son Samuel was born in Ft. Worth Texas, U.S.A. in 1968 and taken to Beirut when he was two months old. When the Lebanese war broke out in 1975, we were caught up in that bitter struggle between the various factions of the religious and ethnic groups. My son, like many others, lived through the horrors of that war and witnessed the deaths of his friends and grandmother.*

*As the war intensified and our home destroyed, we became concerned for his safety and in 1986 felt it necessary to send him to live with relatives in Richmond, Virginia. He quickly adapted to this new environment, but continued to relive the indescribable horrors of the war.*

*On September 14, 1988 he became so distraught that he entered a military recruiting office in Richmond with a gun and detained eleven persons for several hours. During this episode no one was threatened and no one was injured. Unfortunately it attracted many onlookers, news reporters and television crews.*

*This adverse publicity was sensationalized by the television and radio broadcasters who consistently referred to Sam as the "LEBANESE GUNMAN HOLDING HOSTAGES."*

*In view of this wide coverage by the news media, it was decided not to give him a jury trial. At his hearing were several witnesses, three psychiatrists, his parents, two defense attorneys, prosecuting attorney and the Judge. The prosecuting attorney had little difficulty in obtaining a conviction and a 25 year prison sentence.*

*There is no question of Sam's wrongdoing, but the severity of the sentence and several aspects of this case require re-evaluation:*

*He was defamed as a "LEBANESE TERRORIST."*

*The prosecuting attorney and Judge failed to consider his mental state at the time of the offense.*

*The prosecuting attorney ignored the opinion of the three psychiatrists who stated that Sam was suffering from a "POST TRAUMATIC DISORDER BROUGHT ON AS A RESULT OF THE LEBANESE WAR."*

*Favorable comments by several defense witnesses were ignored.*

*Most important was the banning of a tape showing the killing, bombing and destruction of Beirut, some of this by the U.S. Battleship New Jersey. This tape was considered crucial to Sam's defense.*

*Mr. Prime Minister, my son entered the recruiting office to call attention to the war in Lebanon, and after his message was read over a local radio station, he surrendered peacefully to the police. He is now incarcerated in the Southampton Correctional Center in Capron, Virginia under the Number 167715.*

*Sam is a quiet, non-violent person guilty of nothing other than being a Lebanese-American suffering from a severe stress syndrome. In view of this I am requesting your intervention in obtaining a reduction in his sentence or have him released under house arrest whereby he could continue his college education. The U.S. Secretary of State, Mr. James Baker, U.S. State Department, Washington, D.C. 20520, may be instrumental in helping with this request.*

*Returning him to his parents may prevent him from becoming a hardened criminal and permit him to return to a normal life with limited restrictions. I would appreciate any action you may take on Sam's behalf and trust the situation in Lebanon may soon be resolved so we may return to our home in Beirut.*

*Sincerely,*

*Toufic Deeb Eloud*

My dad was not the only one who took up my cause. A local community activist, Mr. Robert Alan Hay, sent the following letter to Mr. Walter Stosch, a representative in the Virginia House of Delegates, in which he used my case to rally for reform of the assessment methods of state judges, sentencing guidelines, and the parole system.

Mr. Ray wrote on January 9, 1990:

*Dear Walter:*
*As a member of the House of Delegates, you must be as deeply concerned as I am with our horrendous crime rate and our overcrowded prisons. The crime rate will continue to rise until the illegal drug problem is brought under control. Overcrowding however, has much to do with the assessment practices of our Judges and the lack of guidelines for more uniform sentencing. There is, in addition, the age-old problem with our parole system. According to Parole Board Chairman, Clarence*

Jackson, *"The parole board does not have a systematic parole process that leads to uniformity across the board."*

*I feel strongly about the sentence handed down to young, mild-mannered Samuel T. Eloud; his case is typical of the sentences given many of our first offenders and it is not uncommon to have them returned to our society as hardened criminals because of the unfairness of our system of justice.*

*Any action you may take to help correct our existing laws would be appreciated by our taxpayers. You or your colleagues are welcome to review the tape that may have avoided the long prison term given this young victim of the Lebanese war.*

*Sincerely,*

*Robert Alan Hay*

# Chapter 40
## A Bug in My Ear

When I returned to my dayroom after the trial, everyone was happy for me and told me how lucky I was to have only gotten a twenty-five year sentence instead of one hundred and twenty-four. Thankfully, the eight and half months prior to my sentencing would count towards time served.

One day on my way from the kitchen back to my dayroom, I received the usual pat-down. One of the female guards walked up to me and whispered to me that she wanted to put a bug in my ear. And since I didn't know slang, I said, "No, thanks. I don't like bugs!"

I headed on to the dayroom as she gave me a puzzled look. After telling one of the other inmates what had just happened, he started laughing and said that she just wanted to tell you something. So I went back to the bars and got her attention by waving my arm out into the hallway. I told her that I would like to know what that bug was. She smiled, got close to the bars, and said that Monday I would be leaving.

Inmates are not told when they are going to leave for security reasons. Phones were turned off in the dayroom whenever transfers were being made from one facility to another. I thanked her and went to the pay phone to make a collect call to let my mother know that I was going to be transferred on Monday and not to come to see me at the jail. I threw away extra things that I didn't think I would need.

When Monday morning arrived, I saw the others who would be coming with me. There were six of us, three to a police car. We knew each other, having spent eight months together at the Henrico County

Jail. We were nervous about going to a new facility because of stories we heard from others about those places. But, we were glad that we all knew each other well.

The white inmate that rode with me was in for murder and would be in there quite a while. He was young and clean cut. The third inmate was a Latino nicknamed Ponch because he looked like that character on "CHiPs." We all three were shackled together. We asked the officer to loosen up the handcuffs as they were cutting into our wrists. After complaining for ten minutes, he decided to loosen them up a bit because he knew we would complain all the way to our destination, two hours from Richmond. The other three inmates were ahead of us in the other car and we stayed behind them.

Before leaving Henrico jail, an older black man that was the barber there pulled me aside and said, "Don't worry about the penitentiary. It is better than jail." He looked at me seriously and told me as long as I stuck with these three rules, my time would be easy:

Rule #1: Mind your own business no matter what is going on. If it doesn't pertain to you personally, don't comment or say anything.

Rule #2: Do not gamble.

Rule #3: Stay clear of the gay inmates.

Then he gave me the "brother" handshake and told me that I would be fine there.

I made sure I had all my news clippings and articles that had been published because I figured as soon as people knew why I was in there, they would know how crazy I was and wouldn't bother me.

On our trip to the penitentiary, the three of us in the car made a deal that we would stick together and also try to find others there that we had known in jail. We were also told that you will always see someone you know.

After the long ride, we noticed that the scenery started to change; everything got flatter and all we could see were fields of corn, soybeans, and peanuts.

I asked the driver, "What's up with this farmland?"

He said, "Might as well get used to it now because that is all you are going to see until your time is done."

After eight months of seeing nothing outside and not even being able to feel the fresh air, it was nice to see wide open spaces with cows lumbering across the fields. It was like watching a movie for the first time. The scenery was a visual luxury and we could see for miles. In jail, we only saw walls and bars, but here we would feel the rain, the fresh air, and an abundance of sunlight.

As we arrived, we saw that we were in the middle of nowhere, the penitentiary sitting by itself in a field. From the penitentiary you could see the cornfields and cow pastures. At the far end of the pastures was a line of trees around the property. There were double fences with shiny razor wire looking as if it had been freshly polished. It reminded me of the razor wire around the American Embassy in Beirut.

We parked in a small lot in front of the administration building which was connected to the prison itself. I remember seeing the American flag and the Virginia state flag whipping in the wind and hearing the pinging of the cables against the flag pole.

We did our chicken walk with our shackles and handcuffs through the first set of security doors. Once inside the building, the door secured behind us, the officer turned in his paper work showing that he had safely transported three inmates.

Once the paperwork was looked over and our names were confirmed, the officer took the cuffs and shackles off the three of us. It was a very noisy process, the chains clinking against one another. He carried the heavy pile of chains, wrapped spaghetti-like in his arms, back to the patrol car.

We were then escorted through the main doors that separated the administrative offices from the correctional facility. Once the doors slammed behind us, we knew we were in for the long haul.

We walked to the receiving area where an African-American officer went through our belongings removing anything that wasn't allowed there including a ten dollar bill that I had. He added it to my canteen account. After repeatedly asking me where I got the cash, my answer was "It was the white man's fault." And then he laughed as did the other inmates around me. He also asked if we had any tattoos and if so, where and what they were.

After that process was over, we were issued our prison blue jeans, a blue button-up shirt, and our state boots, which looked like cheap brown work boots. Also, we were given a towel, a wash cloth, and two pairs of underwear. We were given a strong body wash/shampoo made for delousing and were sent to the showers before changing into our new prison garb.

We then walked from processing to get a photo ID made, a moment that made me chuckle as it reminded me of Al Capone in the old movies where they took both a front and side view while the prisoner held up his inmate number.

We all knew that we would get numbers in the same sequence with only the last few numbers being different. A lady in that department filled out our paperwork while a nerdy looking inmate prepared to take our photos. He was nicknamed Radar because he not only worked on the radar while on a Navy ship, but he also looked like Radar on "MASH." I had a cigar in my hand when I held my new inmate number up to my chest for the photo. When Radar said the cigar was blocking the numbers, I quickly stuck the cigar in my mouth as he snapped the picture. Later on, after the lady saw the picture as it was being developed, she called me back to have my picture retaken without the cigar, saying that I had only been there one day and had already started with my shenanigans.

We were escorted to our wing. The wings, A, B, and C, formed a cross with a control room in the center. The control room was surrounded by steel bars and Plexiglas with an officer inside who could see all wings from his position. He looked like he was sitting in a cockpit with green and red lights and switches across a control board. The green light indicated that the cell was secure; the red indicated the cell door was open.

We walked by the control tower as we headed toward B wing where I was assigned to cell B-5T, top bunk. As they buzzed the door open, I walked into my new home and a short, chubby, African-American kid wearing thick glasses stepped out to see what was going on.

The guard told him to get back into his cell and he did. He seemed happy that he was getting a roommate as he had been there for days by himself. He introduced himself as "Sewers."

"What's up with 'Sewers'?" I asked.

He said his job before jail was cleaning sewers.

He asked me what my name was and I said "Lebanon," one of several nicknames I had been given in the Henrico jail, the others being "Rambo," "The Beast from the East," and "Freedom Fighter."

He asked what I was in for and instead of going through the whole scenario, I reached into my bag and handed him one of the news articles about the recruiting station. He seemed amazed to have a roommate with such a serious charge and a highly publicized case. He started banging on the cell door while asking if he could let other people read it thus making it easier for me to make it known who I was and why I was in there. I agreed so that people would know that I was in there for a serious crime, but I was not a drug dealer, thief, or child molester.

The guy mopping the hallways at the time came to our cell to get the article and pass it around after he read it. You could hear him exclaim

"Oh, my God. You have to read this" as he passed it on to each inmate. He said we have a true "Rambo" among us.

Within a couple of hours, everybody was banging on their doors saying "Hey, Lebanon, I want to ask you something." They wanted to know how much time I got because they had seen the news reports about the hostage taking at the recruiting center on the local TV channel. Then I heard a voice I recognized yell to me and I realized that it was one of the inmates in isolation that I had given cigarettes to at the county jail. He was glad I was on the same wing with him and he notified all the other brothers that I was cool because I risked my trusty status by smuggling him more than three packs of cigarettes in the month that he spent in isolation.

In prison, very few people used their real names. Instead, they used names like Shorty T, Little Red, John-John, Sugar Bear, LSD, Virginia Beach, Richmond, Ray-Ray, Boo-Man, D.C., Frenchie, and Frisbee.

Frisbee was heavily medicated on Thorazine, a medication that made him drool. The only good thing about being on Thorazine was that he got an extra scoop of food when he went through the chow line.

He knew all the lyrics to the AC/DC songs even though he was a light-skinned African-American. Frisbee asked me to exchange some of his pills for cigarettes after I had been there a while and had gotten a job in the kitchen. After not taking his meds for a while, things started to change, things I will tell you about later.

Unlike the county jail, there was no air conditioning in the penitentiary except for the medical department where there were two ladies named Ms. Ricks, or Hard Times as she was called, and Ms. Pastel, who had a fiery attitude and a distinctive voice.

It was over 100 degrees in the cells with windows opened and no breeze. The steel doors made the area even hotter. While it was good for weight loss, it was not good for sleeping. The only time you could get any sleep was between two a.m. and five a.m. So while lying in our bunks, you could always tell it was hot because everyone was quiet, the heat draining our energy.

One night, out of the blue, I decided to howl like a wolf. I was good at it and it was very loud, making my roommate jump out of his bunk and ask me "What the hell is wrong with you?"

To spite him, I did it one more time and within one minute the two inmates in the cell next door started barking. A chain reaction began and barking was heard all the way down the hall and back. It was the loudest barking you could hear. The fat inmates had big, deep barks and the skinny ones had smaller barks. My roommate started to laugh and then joined in the barking. The barking was now coming out of thirty-five cells from seventy inmates. It was so loud that the guards came running down to see what was going on.

To our surprise, the guards started laughing while they were writing in their log books what was happening. After twenty minutes of continuous barking, the penitentiary sounded more like a kennel than a prison with many species of dogs, from pit bulls to Rottweilers, German Shepherds, and Doberman Pinschers.

Once things had been quiet for a few minutes, a single, sharp, yippy bark broke the silence once again. A gay inmate two cells down from me began barking like a little Chihuahua causing the whole inmate population to erupt all over again, but this time barking deeper and louder than before. Silly it was, but it provided entertainment, a kind of comic relief from the life we led as prisoners.

The next morning when we were out in the yard playing basketball, volleyball, horseshoes, or lifting weights, everybody was joking about the barking the night before. The barking became an afternoon ritual for a while when we were returned to our cells after being outside for two hours of recreation.

* * *

I tried to play horseshoes one day and when it was my turn, I overthrew the shoe and it landed on the basketball court. One of the inmates advised that I should throw it the way we throw grenades in Lebanon, but instead of overhanded to throw it underhanded. Doing so improved my game and I became good at horseshoes.

I always had an interest in weightlifting, but when I attempted to lift weights, I was quickly out of breath and my arms felt like jello. So, I asked the biggest guy at the weight pile how come everything was so heavy and I was getting tired so quickly. He asked me if I smoked and I proudly said yes, a pack and a half a day. He said when I decided to quit smoking to come and see him.

That afternoon, when I finished my last pack of cigarettes, I decided to quit cold turkey. I felt sick for a week, like I had the flu. I went back to the weight pile and saw my friend who was called Delaware. I told him I had quit smoking and he smiled and said that now I should start doing pushups in my cell.

Within a few weeks, I could do thirty pushups at a time with my feet hooked over the edge of the sink. My strength doubled. After that, I started lifting regular weights and quickly began gaining muscle. I felt strong and had lots of energy, making it more difficult for me to sit calmly in my cell. So, I started to take books from the library, stuff them in a pillow case, and use them to do arm curls.

When there was a shakedown, the officer, seeing all the books in my cell, complimented me on my extensive reading. His name was Mr. Epps, a very nice officer who treated everyone with respect, something that is unusual in prison.

The officers entered the cells, morning and evening, and with a special hammer they would bang on the window bars to the outside to make sure that they had not been tampered with, creating a funny rhythm we came to expect every day.

One morning, I had overslept and was still in my bunk when the officers came in to sprinkle cleaning powders in the cell sink and toilet for us to clean. When my roommate told them I was still sleeping, one officer, a former Marine who served in Vietnam, said "I know how to get him up."

He yelled, "Hey, Lebanon. The Israelis are coming!"

Before he could finish his sentence, I had jumped off the top bunk and landed on the floor.

He, too, was a nice officer. I asked him if he knew if I could get a job there. He said my best bet was to ask Ms. Jones, who was the kitchen supervisor. I also asked if he could put in a good word for me because I had experience making pizzas at Leonardo's and had worked at the kitchen in the county jail.

One day as I was going through the chow line, Ms. Jones happened to be supervising the line, making sure the people working on the line gave the proper amount of food and not too much to each inmate. I asked her if there was an opening in the kitchen because I was interested in working. I let her know I had done kitchen work at the jail and had survived pots and pans. She smiled and said "I'll keep you in mind."

After a few weeks of boredom, some kitchen workers were transferred out to other facilities and I was called out of my cell to meet with Ms. Jones in the kitchen cafeteria. She asked me about kitchen work at the jail and also about my work experience at Leonardo's. She told me I would have to get up every morning at 4:00 a.m. I told her that was not a problem for me. It seemed to be her main concern.

Late that afternoon, my cell door buzzed open, and as usual my roommate and I came out to see what was going on. We noticed an officer, Officer Parker, better known as Flatfoot, walking towards us with kitchen whites in his hands. He wobbled from side to side because of his severe flat feet. He was a cool guard that didn't care about anything that was going on with the inmates as long as nobody was fighting. He handed me my kitchen whites and he said, "Welcome to the jungle." The jail had been the zoo; now I was in the jungle.

My roommate was not happy that I got a job in the kitchen because he had nobody to talk to until I got back from work. Kitchen workers or any workers got to come out every night to watch TV while wing inmates could only come out on certain nights.

I was glad to start working in the kitchen and pots and pans was always the first assignment, just like in the county jail. The good part was that I got as much food as I wanted, my number one priority, and whenever a kitchen employee got transferred, you could move up and someone else would take your position. I only had to stay with pots and pans for three days before moving up to the handyman job. I swept the dining room, brought out trays from the dishwasher to the line where I stacked them up, and unloaded trucks bringing in food supplies.

While working in the kitchen, I came up for parole for the first time. Usually the parole board process began when one person visits you in jail with his laptop and asks questions about the crime you committed, the most important question being "Why should we let you out?"

I met with my first counselor at the penitentiary, Lazy Leonard, a nickname given to him by the inmates. He tried to give me tips on what to say in my parole meeting including what I had accomplished during my incarceration.

Every inmate that had anything to do with Mr. Leonard complained about how unhelpful he was. Understand that when you are incarcerated you learn to read people very quickly. Within a few seconds of being around someone, you can know so much by their body language and the first few words out of their mouths.

The folks in the barbershop, including my friend D.R., had labeled him as L.L., which in prison terms meant double larceny. He wanted to be cool with everybody and never really did his job as a counselor.

Lazy Leonard, or L.L., was also known as Bad News Leonard because he delivered the parole rejection letters. In all my years at the penitentiary, not one person had a good thing to say about him. In fact, not one of the inmates he counseled was paroled and I was to be one of them.

After meeting with the parole board and talking about my crime, they said they would get back with me in a few weeks. They did. I saw Bad News Leonard coming down the hallway with a letter in his hand and that was when I knew that I was being turned down. He asked if I wanted to talk to him about it and I replied, "No. I just want the letter."

Now I knew that I had six months before my next parole hearing. Booker, a fellow inmate who worked in Receiving, had spent twelve years in prison, and had experienced many parole hearings, offered me some advice. He told me to write them back and tell them that the serious nature of the crime was never going to change whether it was thirty years ago or a week ago. Then, they would not be able to use that argument to turn me down again, much better advice, as it turned out, than any I ever got from my counselor, Lazy Leonard. Needless to say, I asked for a new counselor.

# Chapter 41
## Frisbee

One day after work around 2:00 pm, I went outside to lift weights. Now I was able to lift twice as much weight and was gaining muscle.

While standing outside on the slab of concrete lifting weights, I heard the familiar sound of a jet fighter bearing down on us. I quickly dropped the weights out of my hands and dove into the dirt. Everybody stopped what they were doing to look at the jet fighter and then at me. I was covered in dirt and everybody started to laugh. The jet had come so low that you could see every detail on it. The officer watching us in the rec yard who had served in Vietnam started to laugh and pointed towards me saying I was still in shell shock from the war.

Apparently, that observation was recorded and a psychologist was assigned to me because even though it was funny, it was unusual behavior. The officer also said I needed to get used to it because the U.S. military used installations like the prison as practice for bombing runs.

I sighed and said, "I can't believe this. I was sentenced to serve time not be tortured with the sound of jets flying low overhead," something that happened several times a week.

Inmates began to look at me instead of the jets as they flew over at low altitudes. Every time the planes came over the guards would start giggling.

Every day after finishing my kitchen duties, I would go to my wing, take a shower and a nap, and when I got bored, I would think of the war in Lebanon in great detail. I was so good at visualizing moments in the war that for a few hours every day I completely escaped prison life, those visualizations always in slow motion so I could stretch it out as far as I could.

As I passed Frisbee's cell one afternoon, he asked me if the offer was still good for giving away his meds for some cigarettes. I told him as long as it was safe and the guards were not looking I would do that for him.

Within a few weeks of Frisbee selling his meds for cigarettes, he was no longer drooling and was more alert to what was going on around him. He told me that he had a plan to get himself moved from this facility to a mental institution and then from there he was going home. I asked him how he was going to play crazier than he already was. He said give him a few days and I would see. He was not joking.

As I passed by his cell two days later, he asked me if the coast was clear and if there were any officers around. I looked and nodded that the coast was clear.

He asked me if they were going to let us go home for Christmas. I laughed and said "You see those bars behind you?"

He said, "Yes."

"That is what we are all going to see for Christmas!"

He said "Then I am going to go off!"

He reached into his toilet and pulled out a large turd and smeared it all over the walls while laughing loudly. I started to laugh with him because it was the funniest and nastiest thing I had ever seen. He was drawing flowers and smiley faces with his poop all over the lime green walls. An awful smell spread all over our wing. I acted as if I didn't know what was going on and hustled to the kitchen to get away from it.

Within fifteen minutes, you could hear inmates yelling because of the smell floating down the hall. Once they found out it was Frisbee, people began cursing at him, yelling that they were going to kill him because all of D wing smelled like shit. The guards came to check out the situation and when they saw what was going on, they didn't know what to do. They tried to talk to him through the quarter-size hole in the Plexiglas window in his door. He laughed, got some more shit, and pushed it through the hole in the window. The guards jumped back, still not knowing how to handle him and not wanting to get his shit all over them.

Finally, the prison captain, Captain Sutton, showed up wearing his white shirt with his captain bars on his collar ready to assess the situation. He made a loud comment that Frisbee was not that crazy as he was not yet eating his poop.

When Frisbee heard that, he wiped some shit across his mouth. After doing so, all the guards' eyes widened because they couldn't believe what he had done.

Captain Sutton said, "Yep. That's it. He's crazy."

The guards put on latex gloves and told Frisbee that they were going to take him to the hole in the receiving area which only had two cells with bars and were only used for serious cases like stabbings or suicide attempts.

They asked Frisbee to turn around and they carefully handcuffed him while trying to avoid getting shit on themselves. Frisbee walked away with his head down, a smile on his face.

All the other inmates disappeared back into their cells to avoid being asked to clean up the mess in Frisbee's cell.

Frisbee was escorted to the hole in the receiving area and those two cells looked like old-fashioned jail cells with bars from floor to ceiling. Once reaching the hole, he had to surrender everything, including his clothes. All he had in his cell was a large, flat vinyl bag with little padding in it that served as his bed and the usual prison sandbag pillow. No one wanted Frisbee's old cell because they knew how Frisbee had decorated it even though it was a single cell.

A week later, I was on my way to work in the kitchen when I saw a doom squad, officers in riot gear, running down the hall with their shields and billy clubs raised. They told me to get out of their way.

I recognized two of the officers and I asked them where they were going. They said they were going to beat the crap out of Frisbee.

"Why?" I asked as I walked closely behind them.

We had gotten to the receiving area when we saw that Officer Williams, or Robo Cop as we called him, was physically shaken and cussing angrily. The doom squad was talking to Officer Williams about what happened.

He said that Frisbee threw a piece of crap that skidded across his paperwork at his desk while he was processing some new inmates. He wanted them to beat the crap out of him.

You could still hear Frisbee in the background cussing, yelling, and slurring his words. Right before they went to Frisbee's cell, I asked if I could speak to him just for five minutes before they beat him. They agreed to the five minutes and warned me that he still had a piece of poop in his hands and was ready to throw it.

I told them I would take my chances as I knew Frisbee well. I asked one of the other inmates to let me borrow a cigarette and a match. I started walking towards Frisbee who was still cussing and yelling and threatening the new inmates sitting in the receiving area where a huge fan outside his cell faced the inmates.

Walking with caution towards Frisbee, I smiled and told him I had something for him. He was so irate it took him a few minutes to recognize me. He smiled back, still holding on to the poop in his right hand, his left hand clenching the bars.

I told him he needed to calm down so he could have the cigarette I had for him. But first, he needed to get rid of the poop in his hand, flush it down the toilet, and wash his hands. Then we could talk about what happened.

He was naked and sweating. His bed had no sheets on it, sheets not being allowed in the hole. He sat on the edge of the bunk close to the bars. I handed him the cigarette. His hands were shaking so badly it took two tries before I could light it for him as he held it to his lips. Out of the corner of my eye, I could still see the doom squad waiting in anticipation. After taking two to three drags from his cigarette, he started to tell me the details of what happened.

Frisbee said he was sound asleep with the fan blowing on him. All he remembered was that all of a sudden he was hot and sweaty and someone had moved the fan's direction away from him.

When he started to yell to Officer Williams about who turned the fan, Officer Williams told him to shut the hell up.

When he asked the other inmates in receiving who turned the fan, they wouldn't answer because they were scared and new to the facility.

That was when he threw the poop at Officer Williams, missing him by only a few inches and instead leaving a big brown skid mark on his paperwork, making it look like the end of a runway at a busy airport.

I asked, "That was it?"

He said, "Yes."

So, I stood up from crouching by his cell and turned the fan back into his direction. As soon as he finished his cigarette, he flushed his toilet again and went to sleep.

I walked away from the cell and told the guards, "It's over."

Some of them were disappointed because they were young and wanted some action. An incident report was filled out and late that afternoon the warden came to the kitchen with his assistant after the regular population was fed. He asked me to sit with them and, of course, my first reply was "I didn't do it."

They laughed and said, "No, have a seat. We want to talk to you about something." I was a little nervous because in the past every time I saw a high-ranking official it was because I had done something wrong.

Mr. Diggs, the warden, an elderly man with thick glasses, a paunch, white hair and moustache, asked me to have a seat at the far end of the dining room at the stainless steel tables. Next to him was the assistant warden, an African-American with a bald head and clean-shaven face, wearing a nice dress shirt.

After sitting down, the warden jokingly asked me if I had ducked any planes flying overhead lately. That broke the ice and I knew it wasn't about anything negative.

I jokingly said, "Not today."

He said that he had received a report and heard from other officers what had happened that morning with Frisbee. He was pleased that I took the risk and diffused a situation that could have escalated with someone getting hurt since Frisbee was on heavy meds for his mental illness.

I replied that Frisbee was a nice guy and I was just trying to do the right thing.

The warden said he knew my case very well and he wanted to know if I wanted to stay in the SRCC honor dorm which was upstairs and separate from the population. There each inmate had his own cell with a standard door the inmate could lock and come in and out of whenever he pleased.

He said that he would be taking a great risk because of my "C" custody level, which was for high-risk and serious crimes. I could only go to the honor dorm when I made "B" custody, which was coming up in the next two weeks. If the officers and the counselors agree on moving me to "B" custody, then I could go to the honor dorm. If not, I would have to stay in the same place or eventually move to a different facility.

My new counselor met with me a week prior to my evaluation for suitability for "B" custody. She said I had a good chance of getting it since all my reports were favorable.

To my surprise, a week later I was given "B" custody and was asked to move upstairs to the honor dorm. I grabbed my stuff, excited that now I would be able to come and go from my room, which meant more opportunities to make money.

I waited until the escorting officer was distracted so I could retrieve my shank which was worth at least three cartons of cigarettes. It was very sharp and long enough to do some serious damage. I slid it down the inside of my sock where it stayed upright and walked slowly to keep it from cutting my leg.

The officer asked me why I was walking so slowly and I replied, "I have twenty-five years to go. What's the hurry?"

# Chapter 42
## Tattoos

Once I got upstairs, I was greeted by three of my workout buddies who were happy to have me join them because now we could work out together daily. The workouts took place in the late afternoon as the sun was going down. It was cooler then and the yard was empty of the regular population.

Once I got adjusted to this new housing area, I was able to enjoy some extra benefits: more phone access, unlimited TV, and an ice-making machine.

I found a new hideout place for my shank, something that took a while. It was a small hole close to the showers behind the heating vent. I taped a small string to it so I could pull it from the hole.

While there, I also met a tall, bald-headed inmate called Bullet Head. He looked like the bailiff on "Night Court."

We were watching a movie one night when Bullet Head happened to be seated next to me. During the movie, he leaned over and asked me if I wanted to write to his sister.

I looked at him and said, "What are you, sick? Who would ask a fellow prisoner to write to his sister?"

He burst out laughing and high-fived me. That is how our friendship started.

I asked him about his artwork I had seen in his room. He said that he liked to do tattoos, and of course, you could see he had a few himself. He said that he was trying to get a Walkman to take it apart and get the motor out.

When I asked how he would make the needle, he said he had a small piece of guitar string that when it was unraveled had a sharp wire inside. As for the ink, he said to hand him the deck of cards on the table.

He took two cards and lit one of them on fire while holding the other one over the flame. You could see the black soot accumulating on the top card as he used the top card to catch the soot coming from the burning card below. The ink on the burning card created a lot of soot. After that, he would scrape the soot from the card, mix it with baby oil, and voila, there is your ink. I thought that was very clever and how unbelievable it was that people could be so creative in a non-creative environment.

The next day, I used all my connections and three packs of cigarettes to get a Walkman cassette player. I knew it had to be stolen since no one is allowed to sell their own Walkman or let anyone else borrow it. If you were caught with someone else's Walkman, you were written up.

When I walked into Bullet Head's cell with the cassette player in my hands, his head almost hit the ceiling as he jumped off his bunk. He was like a little kid on Christmas morning.

I told him he needed to ditch the case as soon as he could after getting the motor out because once the guards had been alerted it had been stolen, there would be a shakedown.

Within ten minutes, the cassette player was disemboweled and a few hours later came the shakedown. All the evidence had disappeared, smashed into little pieces and thrown into the trash. After that, it was business as usual.

He used a Bic pen and somehow inserted the guitar string inside the pen. He wrapped some string around the tip of the guitar string needle where it was soaked with the ink mixed with baby oil so it could penetrate the skin more easily.

It didn't take long to find quite a few customers who wanted tattoos. They either had drawings they had done themselves or they wanted him to get creative and draw something they thought was cool. So, I was making three packs of Newports for every customer I brought him. I averaged around three customers a day. Timing was everything because we had to sneak people to the honor dorm before or after count was taken.

One inmate was caught on the rec field because he was showing off his brand new tattoo. It was obvious the tattoo was fresh because his arm was swollen.

It was the funniest tattoo I had ever seen, a huge rat with buck teeth standing on its hind legs with a penis as large as he was and a word bubble over his head that said, "Here Kitty, Kitty, Kitty."

He was escorted back inside the building and was charged with destruction of state property, he being the property of the state. He never told where he got the tattoo which gained him more respect from the other inmates for not telling. He served two weeks in isolation with his rat.

# Chapter 43
## From Inedible to Gourmet

Out of the sixteen inmates in honor dorm, six of us were into weightlifting while everybody else played basketball and horseshoes.

During the summer, as the sun was setting and we were outside exercising, a large bird would fly right over the yard. I would point at him and say, "The crane, the crane."

It was comical because the bird flew over almost every day at the same time going in the same direction. Sometimes you would see frog legs hanging out of his mouth so we knew there was water somewhere nearby.

There were always people yelling from their cells through the bars trying to see if we could lift more weight. Sometimes they would ask what we were having the next morning for breakfast since some of us worked in the kitchen.

After a few conversations with people in their cells, I discovered that one of them said that he had been to culinary school. I didn't know what culinary school was so I asked and he laughed and said it was a school that taught you how to cook.

I replied saying I was a freedom fighter and didn't know anything about cooking.

After thinking about it for a few days and because the food there either had no taste or was just disgusting, I told Ms. Jones about Frenchie, who had been to culinary school and would be a great asset to our kitchen.

After a few days of my nagging Ms. Jones, she told me to go down to his cell and get him. I ran to the control tower and asked the officer to buzz Frenchie's door open because Ms. Jones needed to talk to him. He buzzed the door open and said to make sure I closed it as he watched me go down the hall.

I asked Frenchie to get his clothes on because Ms. Jones in the kitchen wanted to talk to him about a job. He hopped up quickly and put on his smocks. He was starting to fix his hair when I told him we weren't going to a disco, just to the kitchen. I made sure I slammed the cell door behind him and looked at the officer in the control tower who gave me the thumbs up.

Ms. Jones interviewed Frenchie for about twenty minutes and she said the current head cook was being transferred out soon and asked him if he was interested in that position.

Three days later, Frenchie was in the kitchen and within minutes disgusting food was turned into gourmet. It was like Martha Stewart at her peak. Everything Frenchie touched tasted good. The whole prison attitude improved dramatically because of the positive change in the food. People couldn't wait until it was time to eat and on the days when Frenchie was off, few even showed up at the dining halls.

One of the inmates that worked in the kitchen asked me if I was interested in getting in on making homemade alcohol, or mash as it is called in prison.

Even though I was never much of a drinker, I decided to participate because I wanted to learn how you could make alcohol out of what we had in the prison kitchen. He said that the main ingredient was yeast, which was always locked up. The only person that had access to it was Jose, our baker, who had been there since he was a juvenile for involuntary manslaughter during a robbery attempt.

I approached Jose and told him what the deal was. I told him that if the project was successful, we would share the mash with him. He said give him a few days. During those few days, we noticed how flat the bread was. Some people complained, but we knew what was going on so we didn't say anything. Now we had enough yeast to start our mash.

Before we even started the process, we needed to have a hiding place. I was told it would cause an odor once the process had started.

One of my workout partners, an inmate from D. C., discovered the best hiding place which was next to the motor on top of the walk-in freezer. A panel had to be removed for us to store the mash and then replaced which didn't take long and it was easy to get to.

We started by getting a five gallon bucket in which we put a black trash bag, then added the following: oranges, potatoes, raisins, grapes, pineapple chunks, apples, orange juice, and the main ingredient, yeast. Then we tied the bag and stored it over the walk-in freezer.

Every two to three days, the bucket had to be brought down so the gases could be released. The smell was awful so it had to be done quickly before someone noticed. We didn't want the others to know about it as only the few who risked their status and jobs by making it would be allowed to partake. It was Super Bowl season and that is what the mash was for.

I got a t-shirt from Booker who worked in receiving so we could strain the mash to keep the pulp out of the alcohol mixture. It was an easy process. The end product tasted like fruit punch or a Hawaiian cocktail. I was shocked at how good it tasted since I never really liked the taste of alcohol. I asked how something that tasted this healthy and harmless could get us drunk. We quickly smuggled the mash in plastic pitchers to our living area upstairs.

That night during the Super Bowl everyone was glued to the TV and radios. While everybody had a full pitcher, I only wanted a quarter of a pitcher. Within a few minutes of drinking the mash, I began to feel intoxicated. That is when I looked at everyone else and they all started smiling. I couldn't believe that something that tasted that good could have alcohol in it.

That process was only done a few times since the guards caught on because of the strong odor. The only way to minimize or eliminate the odor was to take toilet paper, rub deodorant on it, and set it on fire. The burning toilet paper gave off quickly and strongly the deodorant scent.

That was also used to conceal the smell of marijuana when it was being smoked. Also, Bounce dryer sheets were put inside an empty toilet paper roll and the person smoking marijuana would exhale through the tube with the dryer sheet inside to conceal the marijuana smell.

**Christmas in prison at Southampton Correctional Center
in Capron, Virginia**

# Chapter 44
## Coach

After two years of working in the kitchen, I found out that there was a job opening with Coach in the recreation department.

Even though he was a correctional officer, Coach always dressed in civilian clothes and carried a walkie-talkie. His wife was my counselor at the prison. I wrote Coach a note and told him that I was interested in the job and also notified Ms. Jones, our kitchen supervisor, to put in a good word for me since they seemed to talk with each other often. After the inmate who held that job was released, I was notified that I would get the job.

There was no other job in the whole institution that could have suited me better. Part of my job was to take the weights out twice a day which allowed me to work out twice a day. I had to make sure the weights were counted when returned to the shed room.

Once an inmate had stolen a dumbbell, wrapped it in a towel, and used it as a battering ram to break the bars of his cell, the towel helping to muffle the sound. I don't blame the guy since he was facing forty-six years in federal prison, but his cellmate, who only had six months left, decided to escape with him. While they were crossing the roof, the guards in the building heard their footsteps pounding as they ran across, alerting the guards who intercepted them in the parking lot.

The next morning, the entire prison was on lockdown except for kitchen workers and anyone on the trusty level. The doom squad, consisting of fifteen officers dressed in military-looking attire including combat boots, was patrolling the rooftop of the prison and the perimeter fences to see how the inmates got past the barbed wire.

A blanket had been tossed over the corner of the fence near the rooftop where the inmates jumped off. It was the only spot where the fence was not doubled and had the least amount of barbed wire covering it.

The rest of the compound was enclosed with double fencing, with a ten foot swath of grass growing between them. A few days later, the entire fence was reinforced with new razor-sharp barbed wire. The barbed wire was in big rolls that were stacked on top of each other the height of the fence. We knew how sharp it was because several birds became its victims. You could see them struggling to get out of the wire where they had become entangled. Most of them, like us, were not able to escape, and again, like some of us, died there.

The razors and wire were so shiny that on sunny days you couldn't stare at it but for so long because of the glare from the sun. Now it was definitely a maximum security prison. Also, all the cell bars were replaced by much stronger steel throughout the prison.

I met with Coach for the first time in his small office which had a desk, a phone, and recreation equipment, including basketballs, volleyballs, and a TV and VCR on a rolling cart.

After talking about the job description and what was expected of me, I learned I would cut the grass in between the fences when needed. Cutting the grass between the razor wire fences earned me new shirts at least once a month because the razors caught my sleeves, tearing them.

Another part of my job was to push the TV cart into the movie room adjacent to Coach's office for the inmates who were inside while another group was exercising in the yard. On rainy days, I helped the barber shop by taking a list to the general population and bringing inmates in to have their monthly haircut, if they so desired.

One of the barbers, D.R., an African-American from southeast DC, befriended me and loved my Lebanese war stories, which were some of the many stories one hears in a barber shop. We became friends and started to follow the ongoing news stories about Pablo Escobar's Columbian drug cartel.

Since ninety percent of the inmates were in for drug convictions, Escobar was a very popular topic. Daily news clippings about Pablo were shared among inmates. He was thought of as the Robin Hood of the drug cartel leaders because he built low-income housing for citizens that the government was not able to provide. He even paid off the Columbian government's deficit. We were intrigued by his ability to bribe even FBI and other federal agents into coming on his payroll.

Coach seemed a very quiet person when you first met him. When I asked him why he hired me out of three hundred other inmates, he smiled showing his bright white teeth and said that he never had a celebrity work for him before.

As soon as trust was formed between us, we became good friends. I even helped him study for his volunteer firefighting test for the Boykins Fire Department. I always kept an eye on Coach, especially at the weight pile, in case any other inmates had plans to harm him. Some inmates had not learned how to abide by penitentiary rules and could become agitated when given directions even by mild-mannered Coach.

One morning as we walked out to the yard before the inmates came out, we found a couple of toothbrushes with razors embedded in them. That was a popular, cheap way to make a prison knife, by melting the plastic and embedding the razor in it as it cooled. They had been stuck into the ground to be used in the yard at a later time.

And of course, when the jets flew by and even if I was lifting weights, I would still toss the weights aside and dive onto the ground. Coach always got a kick out of that. Everyone else laughed, too.

Whenever the grass needed to be cut in between the fences, I was always glad to be the one doing it so I could get more sun exposure, even when it was 110 degrees and Coach would say we should wait. I would beg him saying that as long as I had a bottle of water, I could do it. I would say it was a beautiful day and he would ask how I could say it was a beautiful day when I was in prison.

We also did maintenance and replaced the basketball nets whenever they ripped. We painted the shuffleboard court with yellow traffic paint. I was told shuffleboard was a game for old folks.

I also had to rake the sandy areas where horseshoes were played. It reminded me of the tennis courts in Lebanon where I worked as a kid, sweeping the courts with the welcome mat.

To me, working for Coach was the best job I could have since I had access to everything in the prison but the front door. It made my time go by faster because each day brought a different job.

I found out that there were a lot of people in prison who were illiterate. One of them, Donnie, happened to be in our honor dorm. I always wondered why he never wrote letters to anyone since most inmates wrote a lot of letters.

One night, while watching TV, a scroll came across the bottom of the TV screen. Usually it was a weather alert. This time it was the football scores.

Donnie jumped up and yelled out "There goes another thunderstorm!"

Everybody laughed, laughed so loud that the guards came running upstairs to see what the commotion was. Once the guards arrived and found out what we were laughing about, they joined us.

Donnie got upset and went to his cell and slammed the door and didn't visit with the other inmates in the commons area for three days.

Finally, he approached me and asked me if I could write letters for him. After a few letters, he started to get return mail which made him really happy. He decided to get his GED, taking the test five times.

One afternoon during mail call, I was called downstairs by one of the mail ladies, Ms. Nasty, who was the most disliked officer in the prison. She was a light-skinned African American who sang gospel songs loudly and constantly. She wore pants that were three sizes too small and went strictly by the rules as to what you could get and what you could not. That included pictures of inmates' girlfriends wearing lingerie.

She called me down to tell me I had to return that pair of ladies' underwear that had been sent to me by one of my girlfriends. I wasn't planning to wear them, only to hang them on the cell wall.

Everyone laughed when they found out what I had to send back. That was when other inmates started to request underwear from their girlfriends, making Ms. Nasty even nastier, since now her work was doubled. She had to open all mail, looking for contraband like drugs, money, weapons, or underwear.

One thing we all laughed about that neither she, the administration, nor the U.S. Postal service found out was that one of the inmates had discovered that if you soaked used or cancelled stamps in undiluted Johnson's Baby Shampoo for a few days, it cleaned off the cancellation marks without damaging the stamps. It was a genius idea that saved folks a lot of money, especially the ones who had no money to buy stamps after using up all the stamps, notepads, and pencils that were given by the Salvation Army prison ministry at Christmas time. Mail kept the inmates sane and gave them a connection to the outside world. That is why no one ever revealed the stamp soaking method.

And as for girlfriends, there was also an incident in visitation. Two different girlfriends normally came to visit me on different days. On one occasion, they showed up on the same day, one leaving as the other came in.

One was Marcie, a girlfriend from my days working at Leonardo's Pizza. The second was my English teacher from J. Sargeant Reynolds Community College with whom I had developed a closeness after going to prison.

The guard inside the control booth at the visitation area knew me well and had befriended me. He was giving me sign language through the control window that there was a second girl coming in, so be careful.

So I told Marcie, the girl I met while working at Leonardo's, that the guard was telling me that our time was up.

On her way out, my college professor, Ms. Willis, figured out who she was, and they started yelling at each other. The Leonardo's girlfriend stormed out of the building and ran into a glass door, witnessed by all the guards and now the word was out that even though Lebanon had been in prison for five years, some girls were still fighting over him. Even the warden commented on it the next time he passed me by.

After I told Coach all the details, he laughed, too, and said "At least, there were no jets flying overhead that day."

# Chapter 45
## Jamaican Revenge

One day when I was manning the weights in the rec yard, I was called in by the psychologist and the assistant warden. I thought it was weird since there were no incidents that I had any knowledge of and I didn't want to be seen by other inmates talking with the psychologist and the assistant warden.

They took me to Coach's office so they could meet with me out of sight of the general population. I immediately used the famous phrase, "I had nothing to do with it," before they even began to question me.

They smiled and said not to worry, it is nothing bad. The assistant warden proceeded to pull out an AK-47 shell casing. He handed it toward me and I used a pencil from Coach's desk to scoop it up like on CSI because whatever the reason was, I didn't want my fingerprints on another AK-47 cartridge.

They wanted me to tell them what was written in Arabic on the back of it. It was Arabic for 1974 and was similar to ones made in the Middle East, which are hard to come by in the states. After translating the numbers into English, I asked them to put in a good word with my parole officer because my hearing was coming up in a few weeks.

I started to talk more frequently with my new counselor, Coach's wife, a light-skinned African American, who was very professional and gave me good advice about my parole hearing. I had listened to her all along and talked to a psychologist weekly and got good reviews for my job performance. I also had stayed out of any trouble and had no infractions. But, that didn't prevent me from making some money by smuggling food out of the kitchen and getting paid for being a lookout while people were gambling.

One night when I called my mom to check on her, I got the bad news that my grandfather had passed away in a nursing home in New York. I was upset, but the more difficult thing was that I couldn't go to his funeral. That would take special permission, paying two guards to escort me, and a custody level of A. Mine was B at the time, having risen from C custody, a level which made it impossible to do anything outside or even work in the prison.

When some of my fellow inmates heard of my grandfather's death, they gave me a condolence card they all had signed. That there was concern expressed by all these tough guys made me know that even in a terrible place like prison, there could be kindness.

Being tough was the only way to survive, something all inmates learned. And letting another inmate put one over on you was something you had to avoid.

Here is an example. Word got out that a Jamaican in the rec yard was looking to fight another inmate who owed him three cartons of cigarettes from a bet on the Super Bowl game. To avoid seeing the Jamaican and having to pay the debt, the inmate transferred to another wing.

The Jamaican, a slim guy, loved boxing. When he would see me working out, he would come by to say how much respect he had for me because of the crime I had committed, the one that sent me there.

Also, while he was working out, he would ask us to jump on his stomach, an ab strengthening exercise. Wearing those terrible, hard-as-a-brick state boots, I could jump on his stomach with both feet, lifting two inches from his stomach between jumps, but it didn't faze him. It must have been an exercise he was used to.

When he asked those of us who were working out what he should do about the debt not being paid, all gave the same answer: "You have to do what you have to do" which meant use any means necessary to get even. In prison, if you get yourself in a situation where people take advantage of you once, others will also.

One Sunday while church services were being conducted, I was returning from visitation with my mother and my brother Dani. I was being buzzed through the doors when the officer escorting me had a call on his radio, a code 1033, meaning assistance needed because of a fight.

Once I entered the hallway to go upstairs to my dorm, there were people running out of the church in all directions. Looking in the doorway, I could see where the inmates had circled what looked like a fight. There was a lot of commotion and guards were running towards the scene.

One of the guards was B.J., a dark-skinned African American woman, who was every bit of six foot four and weighed two hundred seventy-five pounds. The first to reach the scene, she came from behind the two inmates, threw her arms around their necks, and held one inmate under each armpit. Because she was so strong and big, she managed to contain two angry inmates that were trying to kill each other until help arrived, puffing on her cigarette the whole time, her blue shirt pulling out of her waistband as she struggled with them.

The guards finally got it under control. One inmate was taken to the medical facility, his face covered in blood, a big gash extending from his sideburns to his mouth. Next came the Jamaican in handcuffs. The minister, who had been conducting services when the fight erupted, looked pale as they escorted him safely to the administration building. I quickly ran upstairs and warned the other inmates in the honor dorm to get rid of any contraband they had since a lockdown and searches were imminent.

The Jamaican was taken to the hall where Frisbee had been housed. The other inmate was taken to a hospital outside the prison where he received over forty-seven stitches.

I talked with the Jamaican who said he hoped that what he did would be a warning to other people in prison who don't pay their debts.

We exchanged a fist bump, his fist coming through the cell bars as he said in his native Jamaican accent, "Much respect, mon."

When outside the prison, this might not have seemed necessary, but in prison tough circumstances required tough responses. You had to be tough and mean when needed for survival. You could not show your soft side.

# Chapter 46
## January 3, 1994

That night, all three wings, A, B, and C, were on lockdown. The honor dorm was not because we were all workers who helped the prison run.

Now that my parole hearing was getting closer and closer, I had talked to my mother about having Mr. Janus, my attorney, send the parole board a letter recommending my release.

Also, my mother managed to get Leonardo's Pizza to send a letter to the parole board that they would hire me back as a full time employee.

Other people, including girlfriends who visited me regularly in prison, sent in letters to the parole board recommending my release and citing my good behavior while in prison.

My main concern was the staff, including officers and the warden, as well as Coach and his wife, my counselor, who would have more influence on the parole board. I felt confident because having all these folks in favor of my parole was the best I could do.

I decided to shave my beard a few days before my hearing which made Coach happy because he said that with that beard I looked the part, the part of a terrorist.

That was my introduction to Magic Shave, mainly used by African Americans because of their coarse beards. My friend the barber, D.R., coached me through it.

I dumped the powder in a cup, added water to make a paste, not too thin, not too thick. Using a wooden tongue depressor, I scooped the paste out and slowly spread it on my face. The directions said to wait three to five minutes and then remove the paste using the tongue depressor in a scraping motion, rinse the depressor, and repeat.

It was the cleanest, closest shave I have ever had and made my face feel like it had been ironed. Since I left it on longer than recommended, it even tightened my skin making me look ten years younger.

The inmates all gave me advice as to what to say during the parole hearing. We even did a practice run with Booker as my parole officer trying to get me not to say things that might show anger or lack of concern for others. That was helpful because it made me look at it from different perspectives. Since Booker had been through eight parole hearings, he knew every question that could be asked and how they would be asked.

The staff was happy that I was going up for parole and they all wished me luck.

The morning of the hearing I was nervous and had talked to my mother the night before about it. I was the third name on the list to enter the parole room and Coach's wife, my counselor, gave me the thumbs up as I entered the room. To my surprise, there was only one person there with a laptop using the Sergeant's desk.

Wearing my prison blues, my shirt crisply ironed and my pant legs with sharp, sewn-in creases, thanks to my friend who worked in receiving, I sat across from the interviewer.

He asked me what I was in for to see if I was going to change the story. I did not. He smiled when he saw where I had used an AK-47 and he asked me if I was trying to compete with Rambo, which put a slight smile on my face, but only briefly. I did not want him to think that I had enjoyed what I had done. I also added that I had completed all the courses needed and had seen the state psychologist regularly. Everything had been documented by my counselor and my psychologist and my work ethics were documented by Coach.

Also, I reiterated that the serious nature of my crime would always be the same; it would never change. When he asked if I had a job lined-up, I showed him a copy of a letter sent to the parole board from Leonardo's Pizza. Once the interview was over, I shook his hand and left the room.

Later that day, when the staff went to have their lunch in the administration building, word came back by Coach and his wife that the interview went well and that the parole officer seemed positive. I didn't want to get my hopes up, so I kept calm and continued with my heavy lifting workouts. I had called my mother and told her about the meeting and she was hopeful that I would hear something soon.

As prison life went on, I kept to my daily routine to keep from thinking about the parole board's decision. Three weeks after the hearing, I got a bill from Henrico County Courthouse for $4,000 in court costs which I thought was odd since they knew I was still in prison. And then I remembered that the only time prisoners got bills was right before being released.

I was in the dining room on a Saturday evening when mail came to the kitchen. My workout partners and I ate after the general population because we were in the honor dorm. The officer who handed out the mail gave me a funny look and, since the letter was from the parole board, I didn't want others to see it.

I said to him, "I'll open it later. I'm sure it's just another bill from the court."

I could feel my heart racing as I finished eating my food. I ran up to my dorm and inside the bathroom stall and tore open the envelope. I started laughing loudly and a few inmates who were passing by asked what was so funny. Not wanting them to know my news, I told them it was nothing, that I had just had a funny thought.

Slowly, I read the words to myself again just to make sure what I saw was real. The parole board had granted parole and the release date would be sent shortly.

In prison, it wasn't a good idea to tell anyone that you would be leaving soon. People with long sentences would get upset or jealous and could cause problems. I had to make sure that nothing would stand in the way of my being paroled. So, I needed to get rid of all the contraband I had stashed here and there in the prison over time.

The most important was my shank. Since it was very sharp and had a small handle, I sold it within minutes for eight cartons of Newports.

Then, I got rid of all my excess clothing by throwing it into a laundry bin in the receiving area.

I called my mother who, after hearing the news, began to cry and asked me when I was coming home. I told her I was waiting to hear my release date.

Sleeping was difficult because of the excitement of knowing I would soon be home. It seemed as if time stood still, every minute a day long.

Finally, my release date came in the mail: January 3, 1994. That night, while the chow hall was packed with inmates, I stood up on my chair and yelled out as loud as I could Martin Luther King's famous words used by all inmates preparing to go home:

"Free at last, free at last. Thank God Almighty, I'm free at last!"

Everybody jumped up, some saying the parole board had to be crazy to let me out while others wished me luck, gave me the old penitentiary handshake, and asked me to stay in touch.

I couldn't sleep for the three days prior to my release. I cut out all illegal activities and gave my address to all the people that I wanted to stay in touch with.

The honor dorm seemed quieter than usual, something that happens when one member of the group is leaving. We had all been together for four years and had become like family. We were a "band of brothers." My workout partners in particular were sad that our last workout together was coming up.

My workout partner, Bam Bam, had a bet with me to see who could lift three hundred and fifteen pounds on a bench press. He said he had done it before, but since I didn't see it, it didn't count - another prison rule.

We went to the rec yard the night before my release and as the sun was setting, our friendly crane flew over the rec yard in his usual flight pattern, over the fence, barely missing the razor wire, and flew right over us as everyone yelled, "the crane, the crane." I knew this would be my last time seeing the crane, which was part of our daily prison life.

We had inmates cheering us from their cell windows. It was very cold that night, so I had rubbed Ben Gay on my upper body. As the lifters were all shirtless, you could see steam rising from their torsos, the steam rising through the security light's rays.

Bam Bam went first while people were yelling encouraging words like, "You can lift that shit, Bam Bam."

With another inmate on one side of Bam Bam and me on the other, we simultaneously lifted each end of the bar and handed it to Bam Bam, not letting go until he said he was ready. He grasped the bar, hands evenly spaced using the markings on the bar.

Once he gave the okay, we both released the bar at the exact same time, being careful not to let it wobble. More shouts came from the windows as Bam Bam took two short breaths and brought the bar down, touching his chest, and then pushed the bar back up entirely on his own.

Once he locked his arms up and said, "Take it," we grabbed each end of the bar and safely returned it to the rack. There were more cheers from the cells and then it was my turn.

Some inmates began barking from their cells just to give me more encouragement. Motivated and excited because I would be leaving the next day, I quickly got on the bench, steadying myself to grasp the bars as they were handed to me, quickly saying, "I got it."

I took a deep breath and brought the bar down to my chest and back up and before they could take the weights, I said, "Let me try one more," since it felt much easier than I thought.

After lifting the second time, more cheers, yells, barking, and banging on the bars came from the inmates. My workout partner and I were glad we had met our goals. That was the heaviest weight I had ever lifted without getting an injury.

# Chapter 47
## Saying Goodbye, Again

Walking away from the rec yard was the beginning of my walk towards freedom. The guard in the tower yelled at me and said, "Good luck, Lebanon. I hope I never see you back in here again."

We were patted down at the door as usual and the guard said, "I heard you're leaving tomorrow. Good luck."

Once inside, I made a collect call to my mom. She said she would be there between 8:00 and 9:00 in the morning to pick me up.

I gave away the rest of my belongings, except eight brand new round neck tee shirts, everyone's favorites. They were tight fitting and well-constructed. After being in prison for almost six years, you learn the difference between a good tee shirt and a bad one. I thought to myself, what would be the best way to take those tee shirts with me. After a brief discussion with four of my honor dorm roommates, they said if I could pull it off, it would be one way of getting back at the justice system.

That night, I couldn't sleep, and I could almost hear the clock ticking the time away. I decided to put all the tee shirts on first thing in the morning before chow time. I was up at four in the morning and the guards on the midnight shift came to say goodbye, shaking hands with me, something that never happens in prison.

I could barely eat breakfast, even though I was hungry, because I had butterflies in my stomach and was excited about leaving. People from all three wings congratulated me and told me not to pull off another Rambo. They said you made your point; now it is time to move on.

With a lot of high-fives and handshakes, I quickly went upstairs to grab my belongings including a whole bag of cigarettes. Stopping at the barber shop located in the hallway towards the administration building, my friend D.R., who kept me posted on news about Pablo Escobar's adventures, gave me a big hug and said, "I hope we see each other again someday."

It was very quiet when I walked away from the barber shop. I headed two doors down to say goodbye to the nurses, Hard Times and Ms. Pastel. Coach walked into the medical department and said that my mother had arrived but it would take a few more minutes to process my paperwork.

I gave him a crazy look and said, "They need to hurry up the paper work before I climb over the fence."

The ladies in the medical department were happy and sad at the same time knowing I would not be making my daily visits to check on them. They were like stepmothers to me, giving me advice on life and taking good care of me physically when I needed medical attention, not just handing out the usual bag of ice and two Tylenol, the cure for everything in prison.

Next I went to the kitchen to see Ms. Jones. She came to the door wearing all white with a cigarette hanging out of her mouth and yelled out, "Eloud, are you leaving?"

I nodded and said, "Yes."

I leaned inside the door and gave her a hug. She told me, "No more taking hostages" and started to laugh. She asked me to keep in touch by calling the penitentiary and asking to be transferred to the kitchen, something I did many times after I was released.

Once my goodbyes were done, my brain was focused on the front door of the penitentiary. While I was waiting at the front door, Coach was buzzed through the steel doors.

He said, "Are you ready?" and I said "I was ready three days ago."

He walked me through the doors and down the administration hall where my mother was standing, my paperwork in hand, chatting with the staff. The staff in administration shockingly was very nice and affectionate, all giving me hugs and shaking my hand, a side of them I had never seen before.

B.J. was teary-eyed when she told me that she never wanted to see me in this place again. I didn't know whether to give her a hug or just shake her hand, but she grabbed me with both arms and pulled me towards her. I was hoping that she wouldn't notice the eight round neck tee shirts I was wearing, but she didn't. I promised her that I would never be back there. I'd be in a pine box first.

My mother gave me a hug and Captain Sutton shook my hand and Coach said he would walk us out. I said goodbye to his wife and thanked her for guiding me through six years of prison.

Once I stepped out of the prison into the parking lot, I could smell the fresh, clean air and could see the American flag and the Virginia State flag whipping through the wind, snow all around us.

My mom got into her new black Honda Accord while I put my stuff in the back seat. Coach gave me his phone number on a piece of paper and said that in twenty-some odd years, he had never given an inmate his home number. I shook his hand and then he gave me a long hug. After being together daily for four years, we were more like father and son.

I got into the car, noticing the radio, steering wheel, and all the gauges while putting on my seat belt. This Honda was so different from the white VW bug our family drove through the cratered streets of Lebanon that my senses were overloaded.

As my mom was driving and talking to me, I was distracted by the outside world passing by. It was as if I had never seen a tree before or a McDonald's, which after six years of prison looked like gourmet to me. I had a list of things that I wanted to eat, but didn't have the appetite to do so because I was so excited and happy to be free.

I leaned back in the seat, a seat that felt like a waterbed compared to the steel bench and the hard cot I had become used to. As we pulled out of the parking lot, I could barely hear my mother's voice as I watched a strange yet once familiar world pass by.

Empty fruit and vegetable stands lined the snowy shoulder of the road. But I could see fresh apples, peaches, tomatoes, corn, yellow squash, pecans, and walnuts spilling out of the bins. I could see my grandmother's garden in Lebanon, the one my dad and uncles tended so carefully. I closed my eyes and for a moment I was standing in a breadline with my brother Wess. Opening my eyes I remembered that here there would be no breadlines. Instead there would be shelves lined with bread, vegetables on beds of ice, fruit of every kind, and meat counters overflowing with steaks and lobster. I could taste them.

I tilted my seat all the way back and pictured myself lying down and falling asleep in my own bed. I could smell the perfumed letters that were stuffed in my bag in the back seat and realized, too, that the touch of a woman would no longer be a fantasy.

# ACKNOWLEDGMENTS

Having lived the first seventeen and a half years of my life in war-torn Lebanon, I found myself frequently telling stories of my childhood and how my family managed to survive those terrible years. Many of those with whom I shared my stories encouraged me to write a book. I knew I needed help putting my stories to paper, and the only way I was able to finish the book was with the guidance of Brenda Gibrall.

I am so grateful for her motivation, time, and effort. Most of all, I appreciate her trust and kindness while she worked with me over the course of a year as I told my whole life story. Brenda is a wonderful person, a great mother, and a good friend. There are no words to express my thanks and appreciation.

To my parents who had to deal with my hyperactivity and attention deficit disorder, I say thank you for my upbringing. Most especially, I wish to express my deepest gratitude to my mother, who had the strength and love to overcome the challenges of bringing up three very different little boys in an uncertain and dangerous environment.

To my dear grandmother who was killed during the war and the many Lebanese, whether Christian or Muslim, who gave their lives to a terrible conflict, I send my love. This book is dedicated to all the resilient people who suffered from the war and its immediate and long term effects whether physical or emotional.

To all my friends and family in Lebanon who were a great part of my life and helped to shape who I am today, I say thank you.

In Virginia, I wish to express my deepest gratitude to the Fahed family who took me in as one of their own and to the best attorney in Virginia, my attorney, the late Mr. Murray Janus. May he rest in peace.

And finally, I can never forget the correctional officers, Jackie Robertson (Coach), and his wife, my counselor, who guided me through my six years of incarceration.

Last, but most certainly not least, I sincerely appreciate the wonderful letters from many people that helped me to stay sane and gave me hope.

# ABOUT THE AUTHOR

Sam Eloud still resides in Richmond, Virginia, where he works as a personal trainer. In his free time, he enjoys scuba diving and flying large, unusual kites at the beach

Connect with him on Facebook: at Sam El Oud
or at *For the Love of Beirut*.

Made in the USA
Charleston, SC
13 March 2015